THE MASTERS

A Play

by

RONALD MILLAR

Based on the Novel by
C. P. SNOW

SAMUEL FRENCH

LONDON

THE MASTERS

Produced by John Clements and Martin Landau at the Savoy Theatre, London, on the 29th May 1963, with the following cast of characters:

(in the order of their appearance)

ARTHUR BROWN, the Tutor	*David Bird*
PAUL JAGO, the Senior Tutor	*John Clements*
G. H. WINSLOW, the Bursar	*Gerald Cross*
WALTER LUKE	*Michael Graham Cox*
FRANCIS GETLIFFE	*Geoffrey Lumsden*
CHARLES CHRYSTAL, the Dean	*Peter Copley*
LEWIS ELIOT	*David Dodimead*
EUSTACE PILBROW	*David Horne*
M. H. L. GAY, the Senior Fellow	*Harold Scott*
ROY CALVERT	*Gary Watson*
THE REVEREND ALBERT DESPARD-SMITH, the Deputy Master	*Allan Jeayes*
DR THOMAS CRAWFORD	*John Barron*
NEWBY, the head porter	*Robert Hartley*
R. E. A. NIGHTINGALE	*Bernard Horsfall*
MRS MURIEL ROYCE, the Master's wife	*Cicely Paget-Bowman*
JOAN ROYCE, her daughter	*Julie Webb*
ALICE JAGO, Jago's wife	*Valerie Taylor*
SIR HORACE TIMBERLAKE	*Robert Cawdron*
VERNON ROYCE, the Master	*Richard Hurndall*
BIDWELL, a college servant	*Morgan Shepherd*
STRAKER, a college servant	*Anthony Watkins*

Directed by JOHN CLEMENTS

Designed by HUTCHINSON SCOTT

SYNOPSIS OF SCENES

ACT I

ACT II

ACT III

Time—the present

ACT I

SCENE I

SCENE—*The Combination Room of a Cambridge college. An evening in spring.*

It is a rich, spacious room with four tall windows at the back overlooking a courtyard and a view of the fellows' building opposite. There are doors R *and* L. *A long mahogany table up* C, *in front of the windows has three upright chairs above it, three below it and a chair at each end. A small, circular table for newspapers is in the corner up* R. *In the corner down* R *is a small table used for chess with upright chairs above and below it, and a leather tub chair* L *of it. Three large, comfortable armchairs are* RC, C *and* LC, *with small occasional tables* L *of the armchair* C *and* R *of the table* RC. *Another leather tub chair is down* L. *A writing desk, with an upright chair above it is set at right angles to the wall* L, *below the door. There are built-in bookshelves in the wall* L *of the desk and a notice-board hangs on the wall above the shelves. At night the room is lit by three pairs of electric-candle wall-brackets between the windows, a table-lamp on the table up* R, *a standard lamp down* R *and a table-lamp on the desk* L.

When the CURTAIN *rises, it is a fine evening. The lights are lit but the window curtains are not yet closed. The after-dinner wine and glasses are laid out on the table.* ARTHUR BROWN, *the Tutor, is pacing up and down* R, *smoking a cigarette. He is aged fifty and is a plump, shrewd, kindly man. At the moment, he is greatly disturbed. He looks out of the window up* R, *glances at his watch then moves down* RC. PAUL JAGO, *the Senior Tutor, is seen crossing outside the windows from* R *to* L. *He is in his fifties, a man of deep feeling, exuberant and impulsive. He wears a light coat and hat. After a moment he enters the room by the door* L.

JAGO (*moving above the armchair* C) Arthur!

BROWN (*moving to* R *of Jago*) Ah, Paul. The very man I wanted to see. You've just got back?

JAGO. Ten minutes ago. London's all right for a couple of days, but we wouldn't have wanted more. (*He removes his hat and coat*) You know, Liverpool Street to Cambridge Station is hardly designed to raise the spirits, but the minute you walk through the College gates, the heart lifts.

(JAGO *exits* L, *disposes of his hat and coat and re-enters immediately*)

It's almost a physical thing. Big Ben is supposed to be the most reassuring sight in the world, but give me the porter's lodge and Newby's topper . . . (*He suddenly becomes aware of Brown's manner*) What is it, Arthur?

BROWN. I've just come from the hospital.

JAGO. The Master?

BROWN. Yes.

JAGO. Bad news?

BROWN. I'm not sure. I'm dreadfully afraid so. The doctors are with him now. Pelham-Slade came out while I was there and we spoke for a moment. He didn't say much, but I know him well. I've arranged to telephone at half past. He said they should be through by then. I hope I'm wrong.

JAGO (*moving below the armchair* LC) We all knew it was serious, of course, but . . . Poor man. Poor dear man. Does the College know?

BROWN. Only Crawford and Despard-Smith. They're waiting at the hospital. We agreed to say nothing to the others until it was certain.

JAGO. I'm glad you told me.

BROWN. I did that for a reason. (*He moves down* R *of the armchair* C) Paul, if it happens, you know what it will mean. In a few weeks, a few months at most, the College will have to elect a new Master.

JAGO. We can't think of that, now.

BROWN. I believe we must.

JAGO. It may not happen. There are so many things they can do these days.

BROWN. I wish I thought that in this case. I may be wrong, but if I'm not we could be faced with a rush election. (*He moves to* R *of Jago*) The College is bound to be divided. It's vital to be ready for it.

JAGO. I don't see why we're so bound to be divided.

BROWN. If fourteen men are divided about most things they're not specially likely to agree about choosing a new Master.

JAGO (*moving to* R *of the desk*) The fourteen will have become thirteen.

BROWN. Yes. Paul, I think you know what I'm trying to say. If that happens, will you let your name go forward?

JAGO (*moving to* L *of the table up* C) For God's sake, Arthur . . .

BROWN (*moving up* R *of the armchair* C) One of us will have to succeed Royce. I believe it should be you.

JAGO (*moving to* L *of Brown*) I'm sorry. We must leave it.

BROWN. I'm trying to tell you why we can't.

JAGO. It's hard to take in. You know, Arthur—it's not always been easy between Royce and me. Yet last term he went out of his way to help me. You remember Alice was ill, and I was utterly distracted, a burden to everyone, including myself. Then one afternoon the Master asked me if I would take a walk with him. He wanted to tell me how anxious he was about Alice and how much he thought of her. It touched me deeply. One's dreadfully vulnerable through those one loves. (*He moves up* R)

(*A church clock strikes the half-hour*)

To face page 2—The Masters, Act I

Photo by Houston Rogers

Brown (*moving* c) I must go and telephone. They'll be out from hall in a minute.

(G. H. Winslow, *the College Bursar, is seen crossing outside the windows from* R *to* L. *He is aged sixty and wears his gown and mortarboard*)

Here's Winslow, now. I thought up a pretext to order a bottle— it's best to keep things cheerful as long as possible—break it with him, will you? I shan't be long. (*He goes to the door* L *and turns*) Oh, and Paul, think over what I asked you. It's damned important.

(Brown *exits* L, *leaving the door open*)

(*off*) Ah—Godfrey!
Winslow (*off*) Deserting us, Tutor?
Brown (*off*) I shan't be a minute.

(Winslow *enters* L)

Jago. Evening, Winslow. First out?
Winslow (*crossing to the armchair* c) My dear Jago, when Gay is in reminiscent mood, my digestive powers are strictly limited. (*He sits in his favourite chair, the armchair* c)
Jago (*moving above the left end of the table up* c) A glass of port, Bursar? (*He pours two glasses of port*)
Winslow. If you please, Senior Tutor, if you please. I gather one of us is presenting a bottle. Who is it, do you know?
Jago. Yes, it's Arthur Brown.
Winslow. Indeed. And what remarkable event is our worthy Tutor celebrating tonight? Wat Tyler's rebellion or the anniversary of Trafalgar?

(Jago *puts a glass of port for Winslow on the table* L *of the armchair* c)

Jago. I'm afraid I've spilt some of it.
Winslow. It's so good of you to bring it.
Jago. You got my note on the closed exhibitions?
Winslow. Thank you, yes.
Jago. I hope it had everything you wanted.
Winslow. It may very well have done. It may very well have done. I should be so grateful if you would explain it to me sometime.
Jago. I struggled extremely hard to make it clear.
Winslow. I have a feeling that clarity usually comes when one struggles a little less and reflects a little more.
Jago (*moving to* L *of the table up* c; *with good humour*) Really, Winslow, there are times when you would strain the patience of a saint.
Winslow. That, no doubt, is a pleasure to come.

(Walter Luke *bursts in* L. *He is a young "Redbrick" scientist of twenty-four*)

Luke. Anyone seen Crawford about? Hello, Jago.

JAGO. Luke, my dear boy, how are you?

LUKE. Going mad. (*He moves down* L *of Jago*) Did Crawford dine in hall tonight, Bursar?

WINSLOW. I think not.

LUKE. Damn! I wanted a word with him on this blasted diffraction experiment.

JAGO. Having trouble?

LUKE. I'm stuck to hell. Oh, well, I can't wait now. (*He moves to the door* L)

JAGO (*pouring a glass of port for Luke*) Don't leave us, Luke. Relax a little.

LUKE. No. I must get back to the lab.

JAGO (*handing the glass to Luke*) The lab will still be there in five minutes. Work not going too well?

LUKE. One second I think I'm all set, the next it seems as useless as the great pyramid.

(FRANCIS GETLIFFE *and* CHARLES CHRYSTAL *are seen crossing outside the windows from* R *to* L. GETLIFFE *is a distinguished scientific Fellow.* CHRYSTAL *is the powerful Dean of the college*)

I'm beginning to wonder if I'll ever get the bastard right.

JAGO. Can a scientist explain it to a very ignorant layman? Sometimes talking out a problem helps.

LUKE. I'm not much at talking. I could draw it for you. (*He moves to the desk* L, *sits, puts down his glass, takes out a pencil and sketches rapidly on a piece of paper*)

JAGO. Please. (*He moves to Luke*)

LUKE. Well—imagine that's a beam of Alphas.

JAGO (*encouragingly*) A beam of Alphas. Yes?

(GETLIFFE *and* CHRYSTAL *enter* L)

GETLIFFE (*as he enters; to Chrystal*) Well, that's always the way—but I wish someone would put Nightingale out of his misery.

CHRYSTAL. He's not up for the Royal *again?*

GETLIFFE. Every year, regular as clockwork. He'll never get in but he goes on hoping. (*He moves to* L *of the table up* C *and pours a glass of port for himself*)

(CHRYSTAL *moves* LC)

WINSLOW. I am, of course, very ignorant in matters of science but I've always understood that Nightingale was one of our brighter sparks.

LUKE (*looking up*) Nightingale! Stone the crows!

GETLIFFE. Oh, yes, Luke, he was once. But the spark burnt out. That's probably why he sets such store on being a Fellow of the Royal.

CHRYSTAL (*crossing and sitting in the armchair* RC) I wish to God they'd take him, he might be less hell to live with.

GETLIFFE (*crossing and sitting on the chair below the table down* R)
Well, we shan't have to cope with him tonight, he's down with flu.
(*He studies the chess-board*)

CHRYSTAL. That's a relief.

GETLIFFE. What?

CHRYSTAL. I mean—poor fellow.

GETLIFFE. Now then——

(LEWIS ELIOT *enters* L. *He is in his late thirties and the third year of
his fellowship*)

I've got young Lewis in a tight corner. Let's see him get out of this
one.

LEWIS (*crossing down* R) What's all this? Francis getting above
himself?

GETLIFFE. All right, Lewis, my friend, come and show us what
you're made of. (*He indicates the chess game*) Now—extricate yourself
from that.

(LEWIS *sits above the table down* R *and studies the board*)

LEWIS. Well, let's see. Ah, yes. Anderson—"The Immortal
Partie".

(EUSTACE PILBROW *is seen crossing outside the windows from* R *to* L.
*He is in his seventies, a Left-wing political don, known and respected
internationally. He carries his gown over his arm*)

CHRYSTAL. Getliffe, before Lewis ties you in knots, you did fix
our next feast for May the sixth?

GETLIFFE. That's right. The Commemoration of Benefactors.

CHRYSTAL. I hope you'll make it a good one. I have an important
guest coming.

GETLIFFE. Good work. Who is he?

CHRYSTAL. Sir Horace Timberlake. I expect you've heard of him.

GETLIFFE. Oh, yes. I know Timberlake.

WINSLOW. I am, of course, totally ignorant of these matters, but
I've seen the name occasionally in the financial journals.

CHRYSTAL. He's one of the most successful men of the day.

(PILBROW *enters* L)

He controls an industry with a turnover of fifty million.

WINSLOW. Indeed.

PILBROW. Who controls a turnover of fifty million? (*He moves to*
L *of the table up* C *and pours a glass of port for himself*)

LEWIS. Sir Horace Timberlake. Chrystal's hooked him for our
next feast, Pilbrow.

PILBROW. Has he, indeed? Well done the Dean.

WINSLOW. I should hardly have thought *you* would have approved
of him, Eustace.

PILBROW (*moving to* R *of Winslow*) Wouldn't you, Godfrey? And why not, pray?

WINSLOW. A millionaire with a title?

PILBROW. He's none the worse for that. If *our* ancestors had made enough money, we should have found *ourselves* wearing coronets.

WINSLOW. God forbid!

PILBROW. Oh, I don't know. I should rather have liked to be a peer.

GETLIFFE. A *red* peer, Pilbrow?

PILBROW (*moving above the tub chair* R) Well, of course. Then when Timberlake became a baron we could have had fun in the Lords. But bring your capitalist up to the feast and show him the sights. I'm only sorry I shan't be one of them.

CHRYSTAL. Why's that?

PILBROW. I shall be in Belgrade on the sixth for the Peace International. But I've no doubt the college will do him proud. Better than the poor old Achaeans would have done. (*He chuckles*)

(BROWN *enters* L)

BROWN (*moving up* L *of the armchair* LC) Where do the poor old Archaeans come in?

PILBROW (*crossing to* R *of Brown*) *The Iliad.* Book eleven. I've been reading it again in bed, Arthur.

JAGO (*moving to* L *of Brown; aside*) Well?

BROWN (*aside*) Nothing yet. (*He moves to the table up* C *and pours a glass of port*)

(JAGO *moves to* L *of the table up* C)

PILBROW. Do you know those chaps' idea of a beanfeast? Pramnian wine sprinkled with grated goats' cheese. Oh, can you imagine how *horrible* that must have been! (*He moves, stands behind Lewis and watches the chess game*)

WINSLOW. I'm bound to say I prefer Brown's bottle.

LUKE (*suddenly jumping up*) My God, I think I've got it!

(*There is general reaction*)

Yes, that's it. Blind ass. Thanks, Jago. (*He moves to the door* L) Thanks like hell.

JAGO. My dear boy, what did *I* do?

LUKE. You listened.

(LUKE *dashes out* L)

PILBROW (*to Getliffe*) He's got you there, Francis.

LEWIS (*to Getliffe*) Mate, in three.

GETLIFFE. Well, I'm damned!

(PILBROW *moves to the table up* R, *selects a newspaper, sits* R *of the table up* C, *takes out a pencil and does the crossword.* LEWIS *rises and moves* c, *below the table.* Brown *picks up the decanter, moves to* l *of Winslow, refills Winslow's glass then hands the decanter to Lewis*)

Brown (*indicating the port*) I believe it's your favourite year, Godfrey.

Winslow. Indeed it is. But what remarkable event are you celebrating tonight, my dear Tutor?

(Lewis *pours a glass of port for himself*)

Brown. Why, the remarkable event I am celebrating is the appearance of young Mr R. S. Winslow in the Seniors' match. I know we should all feel that when the bursar has a son at the college and the young man distinguishes himself, we want the pleasure of marking the occasion.

Winslow (*taken aback*) I must say this is handsome of you, Brown.

Brown. It's a privilege. (*He raises his glass*) Gentlemen, the Bursar and his son.

Omnes. The Bursar and his son!

(*They drink*)

Winslow (*touched*) Thank you, Tutor. Thank you all. Of course, he'll never get into the team. He's thought to be lucky to have got this far. Poor boy, it's the only notoriety he's ever likely to have. He's rather a stupid child.

(Jago *moves to the window up* lc)

Brown (*sitting in the tub chair down* l) I'm not prepared to agree. One might say that he doesn't find examinations altogether congenial.

Winslow. One might say rather more than that. However, he's thought to stand a chance of the Colonial Service, if he can scrape a third.

Chrystal. He'll make it all right.

Winslow. Of course, I'm terribly ignorant in these matters, but I never have been able to comprehend why the remnant of our Colonial Empire should need third-class men with a talent for organized sports.

(M. H. L. Gay, *the Senior Fellow, is seen to cross outside the windows from* r *to* l. *He is nudging eighty, sturdy, white-bearded and indomitable*)

However, it's important for the boy's sake that he shouldn't disgrace himself in June.

Chrystal. Don't worry. Brown will get him through.

Winslow. I'm sorry that my family should be such a preposterous nuisance.

(Gay *enters* l)

Gay (*moving to the table*) Do I see nuts and wine? Indeed I do, indeed I do. Capital! Nuts and wine. I must congratulate the Steward. Where is the Steward? (*He moves above the armchair* LC) Ah, there you are, Winslow. I congratulate you.

WINSLOW. My dear Gay, I was a most uninspired Steward and I gave up being so five-and-twenty years ago.

(ROY CALVERT *is seen to cross outside the windows from* R *to* L. *He is aged twenty-nine*)

GAY (*quite unabashed*) Then congratulate the new Steward for me. Tell him from me he's doing splendid work.

LEWIS. A glass of port, Professor?

GAY (*moving to* L *of Lewis*) Thank you. And some of those little munching nuts.

(CALVERT *enters* L *and stands* L *of Gay*)

(*He looks at Calvert*) Now, what's your name, young man? Don't tell me. "Calvert." Young Roy Calvert.

(LEWIS *pours two glasses of port*)

CALVERT. Good evening, Professor.

GAY. I've got you taped, I've got you taped. Let's see, now, haven't you been deserting us? Where was it you went? Don't tell me. Istanbul. You've been reconnoitring the Turkish museums.

CALVERT. That's right—and the Turkish dancing girls.

GAY. I congratulate you. (*He moves to the armchair* LC *and sits*)

(LEWIS *hands a glass of port to Calvert*)

I was once given an honorary degree of the University of Istanbul. I remember it to this day. I was met at the station by one of their scholars, and his first words were: "Professor M. H. L. Gay, I think? The great authority on the Sagas."

(LEWIS *puts a bowl of nuts and a glass of port for Gay on the occasional table* R *of Gay, then collects his own glass*)

Those were absolutely the first words I heard when I arrived at the station.

WINSLOW. Remarkable. (*He rises, crosses to the bookshelves* L *and selects a book*)

GAY. Yes, indeed. Mind you, I had to demur to the word "great". I said, "Call me the authority on the Sagas, if you like. But without the great." About honorary degrees.

(LEWIS *moves to the chair above the table down* R, *sits and plays chess with* GETLIFFE)

Do you know that I've absolutely collected fourteen of them?

(CALVERT *crosses, stands up* L *of Lewis and watches the game*)

Not a bad bag, eh? From every civilized country except France.

The French have never been able to recognize merit outside their own country. Still, fourteen isn't so bad. And there's still time for one or two more.

Jago (*moving up* L *of Gay; warmly*) I should think there is. And I shall want to present a bottle for every one of them, Gay.

Gay. Make it champagne, will you?

(Winslow *crosses with his book to the armchair* C *and sits*)

I love champagne. Which reminds me. Are any of us publishing a book this year?

Calvert. I may be.

Gay. I congratulate you.

Jago (*crossing to* L *of Calvert*) What's it about, Calvert?

Calvert. "An introductory analysis of certain texts in Middle Soghdian." Catchy title, don't you think?

Jago. I shall look forward to that. Of course, my knowledge of the Orientals is not what it should be, but you have the gift, that's what counts.

Gay. I have a little work of my own coming out. I should not absolutely rank it among my major productions but I'm quite pleased with it as a *tour de force*.

(Calvert *sits on the arm of the tub chair* RC. Jago *stands above Lewis. They watch the chess*)

I shall be interested to see the reception it obtains. I sometimes think one doesn't receive such a fair hearing when one is getting on in years.

Chrystal. I shouldn't have thought you need worry.

Gay. A fair hearing. That's all I've asked for all along, ever since my first book. Ah, my first book. That was a great occasion. When the press told me the book was out, I went round to the bookshops to see for myself. Then I walked out to Grantchester to visit my brother-in-law, Dr Fazackerley—my wife was his youngest sister, you know. And when I told him the great news, do you know that cat of his—ah, that was a cat and a half—he put up his two paws, that cat did, for all the world as though he were applauding me.

(The Reverend Albert Despard-Smith, *the deputy master, enters* L.

Dr Thomas Crawford *follows him on.*

Despard-Smith, *in his sixties, is a morose cleric with a slight stammer.* Crawford, *smooth, impersonal, is in his fifties*)

Despard-Smith (*moving to* L *of Gay*) G-gentlemen, may I have your attention, please.

(Crawford *closes the door.* Calvert *rises and stands up* L *of the tub chair*)

GAY. Clap-clap-clap he went—just like that.

DESPARD-SMITH. Dr Crawford has just come from the Master's m-medical advisers.

GAY. Three thousand pounds I made out of that book. It went like smoke.

DESPARD-SMITH. *Please*, Gay! We have tragic news. Dr Crawford . . .

CRAWFORD (*crossing up* R *of Gay; quietly*) Speaking not as a fellow but as one who was trained as a medical man, I must warn the society that there is no chance at all of a happy issue.

(*There is a silence*)

CALVERT (*presently*) How long?

CRAWFORD. The college must be prepared to have lost its Master by the end of the summer term. (*He moves to the table up* C)

(*There are murmurs from the others*)

GAY. What's this? What's happened?

BROWN. The Master is dying.

GAY. Ah. Indeed. Very sad.

DESPARD-SMITH. It's catastrophic. When Royce asked me to act as his deputy less than two months ago, I fully expected that before the new term began he would be back in the saddle again.

CHRYSTAL. I'm afraid you were the only one who did, Despard. I think we all knew, really, didn't we?

(*There are murmurs of assent.* CALVERT *moves to* R *of Crawford*)

GETLIFFE. Just the same, it's a shock to hear it so soon.

GAY (*munching a nut; comfortably*) Yes, indeed. But I have some recollection the Master had to live on one floor some little time ago.

LEWIS. That wasn't the present Master.

CALVERT. He means Royce.

GAY. Indeed. Royce. (*To Despard-Smith*) You didn't make that clear.

(DESPARD-SMITH *turns away* L *and sits on the edge of the desk*)

But surely Royce is a very young man? We only elected him recently.

WINSLOW. Fourteen years ago last December.

GAY. Ah, well, it will be a sad break with the past.

CHRYSTAL. We've had this in the back of our minds for weeks. Now we know and we've got to face it.

LEWIS (*rising and crossing to* R *of Calvert*) Does the Master know the truth himself?

CRAWFORD (*with a step down*) No. Mrs Royce won't have it. They're bringing him back to the lodge tomorrow. He's not to be told.

JAGO (*with a step in; instantly*) But that's the most appalling thing.

GETLIFFE. You would tell him?

Jago. Without the shadow of a doubt.

Crawford. I'm surprised that you're so certain about that, Jago. I should have thought, "This will mean peace of mind for him for a few more weeks." Let him have it.

Jago. No. That's presuming where no-one has a right to presume. There are not many serious things in a man's life—but one of them is how he shall meet his death. You can't be tactful about death. All you can do is to leave a man alone. (*He turns away* R)

Brown (*rising and moving up* LC) Yes.

Winslow (*briskly*) Yes, well, be that as it may, the sad news we have heard tonight confirms what, as the dean has said, most of us anticipated for some time. Hitherto we have avoided the implications, from a sense of delicacy which I for one have thought misplaced. I suggest that we can no longer do so. Indeed, may I bring it to a point?

Crawford. We should be grateful.

Winslow. I propose, Mr Deputy, that the college hold a meeting forthwith to discuss the vacancy with which we shall soon be faced.

Chrystal (*sharply*) I don't understand.

(Jago *turns away to the window up* R)

Winslow. I thought I made myself fairly clear. I observe we're all here except Luke and Nightingale. Shall we consider ourselves a quorum?

Chrystal (*rising and crossing down* L) One moment. Mr Deputy, I should like us to be reminded of the statute governing the election of a Master.

Winslow. We know the statute. Why waste time?

Getliffe (*rising and moving below the tub chair* R) What's all this, Dean?

(Lewis *moves down* RC)

Chrystal (*firmly*) I should like to hear the statute, please. (*He goes to the bookshelves and takes out a book*)

(Despard-Smith *rises*)

Winslow. Why are we wasting time?

Chrystal (*handing the book to Despard-Smith*) Mr Deputy. (*He sits in the tub chair down* L)

Despard-Smith. Thank you.

(Lewis *sits on the right arm of the armchair* RC. Calvert *turns the centre chair below the table and sits*)

(*He steps forward, opens the book and reads, or rather, half-intones in a nasal voice*) "When a vacancy in the office of M-Master shall become known to that fellow first in order of precedence——"

Gay. That's me. That's me.

Despard-Smith. "—he shall summon within forty-eight hours a

B

meeting of the Fellows. If the Fellow first in order of precedence be not resident in Cambridge, or be otherwise incapable of presiding— (*he shoots a glance at Gay*) the duty shall pass to the next senior, and so on."

GAY. I am, of course, absolutely capable of discharging my duties.

BROWN. We don't want to tire you unduly.

GAY. Tire me, my dear chap? I'm not tired. But our old friend Despard looks a bit groggy. (*To Despard-Smith*) Would you like my seat?

DESPARD-SMITH. No, I thank you.

GAY. You don't want to overdo it, you know. You're getting on. (*To Winslow*) He's getting on.

WINSLOW. Unhappily he's not, but with your permission . . .

DESPARD-SMITH (*reading*) "When the Fellows are duly assembled, the Fellow first in order of precedence shall announce to them the vacancy, and shall cause a notice to this effect to be placed in full sight on the notice-board in the Combination Room."

GAY. Cause to be placed! Cause to be placed! I shall fix it myself.

WINSLOW. Quite unnecessary.

GAY. When the time comes, I shall certainly fix it. I shall also sign it.

BROWN. That's not in the statute.

GAY. Nevertheless, I shall sign it. When people see the signature "M. H. L. Gay", they'll know there's been no hanky-panky.

WINSLOW. Hanky-panky?

GAY. Yes, and no jiggery-pokery, either. (*To Despard-Smith*) Carry on, my dear chap, if you're not too exhausted.

(JAGO *moves down* R)

DESPARD-SMITH (*reading*) "The time regulated for the election shall be t-ten o'clock on the morning of the fourteenth day from the date of the notice if the vacancy occur in term, or on the thirtieth day if it occur out of term." (*He closes the book*) That is the s-statute. (*He replaces the book in the bookshelves then stands below the desk*)

GAY. Fine piece of draughtsmanship, that statute.

CHRYSTAL. Yes, and it makes my point. The college can't take any formal action until the Mastership is vacant.

WINSLOW. Rubbish!

CHRYSTAL. What did you say?

WINSLOW. I said, 'rubbish'. This is formalism carried to extreme limits. I've never known the Dean be so scrupulous on a matter of etiquette before.

(LEWIS *rises*)

GETLIFFE. It's completely obvious the matter must be discussed.

BROWN (*moving to* L *of Gay; smoothly*) I'm sure the Dean never intended to suggest anything else. The little difference of opinion between us amounts to nothing more than whether our discussion should take place at a formal college meeting or elsewhere.

Winslow. Or, to those who haven't the gift for softening differences possessed by the Tutor, whether we shall dissolve immediately into cabals or talk it out in the open.

Getliffe (*sitting in the armchair* RC) Term starts next week. We can't leave things till then.

Winslow. No. Not that the appearance of the men should obstruct the more serious purposes of our society, such as rolling a log in the right direction?

Brown. Before rolling a log in any direction, may I suggest we sleep on it?

Winslow. Brown's universal panacea.

Getliffe. The problem will still be there in the morning, Arthur.

Crawford. Speaking now as a Fellow and not as a former medical man, I consider the College would be grossly imprudent not to use the next few weeks to resolve on the dispositions it must make.

Lewis (*moving a little up* RC) But that's agreed by everyone, Crawford. The only question is, whether a formal college meeting is the most suitable place.

Brown (*moving a little up* LC) I think the Dean and I believe that, with a little private discussion, the College may be able to reach a very substantial measure of agreement.

Calvert. That is a rare and beautiful prospect.

Lewis (*moving to* R *of Calvert; with a grin*) Shut up, Roy.

Getliffe. How do you regard the situation, Mr Deputy?

Despard-Smith. It's nothing short of c-catastrophic.

Chrystal (*stubbornly*) I submit we can't elect while the Master is still alive. (*He rises and moves to* L *of Gay*)

Winslow. And I submit there are certain questions that must be resolved immediately.

Chrystal. Such as?

Winslow. Are we going outside for a Master, or are we going to choose one of ourselves? I think the society will agree there are good reasons for going outside this time.

(*There is a general outburst*)

Brown		My first impression is that I should be rather against that.
Getliffe	(*together*)	Hold your horses! I think we should be careful.
Chrystal		I don't see this college doing that. It always likes to keep jobs in the family.
Lewis		Surely we can find one from among ourselves.

(CRAWFORD *moves to* L *of the table up* C *and pours himself a drink*)

WINSLOW. But if the family lacks a natural leader . . . What is your view, Senior Tutor?

JAGO. I confess I've scarcely given the matter a moment's thought.

WINSLOW. I confess you surprise me.

CHRYSTAL		(*He crosses to* L *of Winslow*) Winslow, this is neither the time nor the place . . .
WINSLOW		Here we are faced . . .
GETLIFFE	(*together*)	Surely the essential point . . .
BROWN		May I suggest . . .
LEWIS		I should say we had a natural leader . . .

(CALVERT *rises*)

PILBROW (*rising and moving to* R *of Lewis; suddenly incoherently, but with force*) No! No, please! Stop! You must! Look here, the College can't possibly have a meeting about a new Master when the man who ought to be presiding is—I mean, for God's sake—I've never known such extraordinary lack of feeling.

(CALVERT *moves behind Winslow's chair*)

| CHRYSTAL | | (*He crosses below Gay to* L *of Brown*) I've said from the beginning . . . |
| WINSLOW | (*together*) | The college must face the situation . . . |

JAGO (*cutting in; with sudden authority*) Gentlemen! The Master of this college is dying. We know that in the coming weeks we must settle on someone to succeed him, however difficult that may be. But surely—surely we can do it in our own way, without utterly offending the taste of some of us by insisting on doing it formally, at a meeting of which the dying man is still the head.

(PILBROW *moves to Jago and pats his arm*)

CALVERT (*moving to the table up* C) That settles it.

GAY. Well said, Jago. I congratulate you.

CHRYSTAL (*moving above the desk*) I have no doubt that we have just listened to the decisive word.

(DESPARD-SMITH *sits in the tub chair down* L. LEWIS *moves to* R *of the table up* C)

JAGO. May I add a personal plea? (*He moves* RC) Forgive me—I make it in the light of past experience. Last time, many of us, myself included, said things that shouldn't have been said. We divided the College. The unity of this place matters more than any one of us. We should do all we can to preserve it.

WINSLOW. A pious, if impractical hope.

CHRYSTAL		It's been made perfectly clear . . .
BROWN	(*together*)	Really, Winslow . . .
PILBROW		Godfrey, for Heaven's sake . . .

Winslow. Permit me to remind you that in every election within living memory, once the knives are out . . .
Pilbrow. Godfrey! Please!

> (*There is a knock on the door* L. *The room is suddenly silent.*
> Newby, *the head porter, enters* L. *He carries his top hat*)

Newby (*to Brown; formally*) A message from the hospital, sir.

> (*There is reaction from the others*)

(*He crosses to* R *of Brown*) Mrs Royce's compliments. She thanks you for your kind enquiry and thought the college would like to know that the Master is comfortable and sleeping peacefully.
Brown. Thank you, Newby.

> (*There are murmurs of thanks from the others*)

Newby (*after a pause*) Will I draw the curtains, gentlemen?
Brown. Please.

There are murmurs of assent from the others. The church clock strikes ten. Newby *puts his hat on the left end of the table, then closes the window curtains working from* L *to* R. *The others settle down to read, to sleep, to play chess.* Despard-Smith *reaches out to the table behind him for a newspaper, and reads.* Brown *sits at the desk and commences to write.* Chrystal *moves to the table up* C *and pours a glass of port.* Getliffe *rises.* Calvert *goes to the table up* R *and selects a paper.* Pilbrow *moves and sits on the chair below the right end of the table up* C *and works at his crossword.* Jago *moves to the door* R. Crawford *moves to the window up* LC *and looks out through the curtains.* Newby *closes the curtains and crosses above the table up* C *to* L *of it.* Getliffe *moves and sits below the chess-table down* R. Calvert *moves, sits in the tub chair down* RC *and reads his paper.* Chrystal *takes his drink and sits in the armchair* RC. Lewis *sits above the chess-table. He and* Getliffe *play chess.*

Newby *collects his hat and exits* L. Gay *sleeps.* Winslow *is seated in the armchair* C. *Everyone but* Jago *and* Crawford *remain quite still.* Jago *moves to the window up* RC, *turns, looks around the room, then looks at Crawford.* Crawford *turns and looks at Jago. He and* Jago *remain looking at each other in the silent Combination Room as—*

the Curtain *falls*

SCENE 2

SCENE—*The same. A week later. Evening.*

When the CURTAIN *rises, the window curtains are closed and the lights are on.* LEWIS *is seated above the chess-table down* R *with a newspaper, working out a chess problem.* BROWN *is seated in the armchair* C. CHRYSTAL *is seated in the armchair* LC. *They are both smoking and are deep in earnest conversation like a pair of conspirators.*

CHRYSTAL. Of course, if the worst happens before the feast we shall have to cancel, but if not, Mrs Royce insists we carry on as usual.

BROWN. In any case, he may put us off at the last minute. He must look on us as very small beer.

CHRYSTAL. I don't think so. He struck me as a man who means what he says.

BROWN. Naturally he'll be staying the night.

CHRYSTAL. Of course. We'll give him the finest room in the College.

BROWN (*sitting up*) I wonder if that's wise.

CHRYSTAL (*sitting up*) You don't think so?

BROWN. I wonder. It could be a mistake to surround him with luxury. A man like Sir Horace might get the wrong idea.

CHRYSTAL (*with a grin*) You mean, he might think we weren't sufficiently poverty-stricken?

BROWN. Timberlake's shrewd. One's got to be careful. Of course, there's no harm in seeing that the room's reasonably decent.

CHRYSTAL. It might be a nice touch to turn off the central heating.

BROWN. And give him pneumonia?

CHRYSTAL. There's always his will.

(BROWN *and* CHRYSTAL *laugh*)

LEWIS (*lowering his paper; amused*) What *is* all this about Timberlake?

CHRYSTAL (*to Brown*) Shall we tell him?

BROWN. Tell him.

CHRYSTAL. There's a chance of a benefaction, Eliot.

BROWN. If it comes off, it will be the largest the College has ever had.

LEWIS. So that's what you're after. How much?

CHRYSTAL. Sir Horace hinted at a quarter of a million.

LEWIS. Phew!

CHRYSTAL (*rising and moving to* L *of the table up* C) He can probably sign a cheque for double and not miss it. (*He pours a glass of port for himself*)

Brown. Timberlake is a very hot man.

Lewis. He must be. How did this start?

Chrystal. He came up for a night last term. Young Timberlake, his nephew, is a pupil of Brown's.

Brown. He's in his third year.

Lewis. Taking Part Two?

Brown. Yes.

Chrystal. I hope to God he gets through. It will shatter everything if he doesn't.

Lewis. Is there a doubt?

Brown. I think he's a shade less stupid than young Winslow, but it's a very near thing.

Chrystal (*moving to the desk and perching on the edge of it*) Anyway, Sir Horace came up and Brown did him well.

Brown. I invited the Dean to meet him at dinner. (*To Chrystal*) You handled him splendidly.

Chrystal. I liked his directness. He said straight out, "Suppose someone wanted to help this college: what do you need most?" So I told him. "Money. As much as you could give us and with as few conditions as you could possibly make."

Brown. He wasn't happy about no conditions. He said he'd have to think about that.

Lewis (*rising and moving above the armchair* rc) How do things stand now?

Chrystal ⎫
Brown   ⎬ (*together*) He's still thinking.

Chrystal. But he's coming again.

Lewis. And bringing his cheque-book?

Brown. That's what we hope.

Chrystal. Of course, by rights, the Bursar should handle this business.

Brown. If he does, it's a pound to a penny he'll put Timberlake off.

Lewis. Yes, just one of Winslow's little jokes and you'd have Sir Horace endowing an *Oxford* college.

Chrystal. We ought to get it unless we make fools of ourselves. But I wish we hadn't got this Mastership hanging over us. It's a perfect nuisance.

Brown. The Mastership matters.

Chrystal. This matters more. Whoever we elect, it will all be the same a hundred years hence. Whereas a benefaction like this— that could affect the College forever.

(Calvert *enters* l *and moves* lc)

Calvert. Oh, Arthur, you asked me to let you know when I'd made up my mind about the next Master.

Brown. Why, so I did, Roy, so I did.

CALVERT. Well, the penny's dropped. I shall vote for Jago. It's all in order. I've slept on it.

BROWN. That's just as well. Because if you hadn't I should certainly have advised you to do so.

(CALVERT *chuckles*)

LEWIS (*moving down* RC) Arthur, I shall vote for Jago, too.

BROWN (*alert*) Well, this is all very interesting—eh, Dean?

CHRYSTAL. Yes. Arthur and I have been turning the matter over. We're inclined to put Jago's name forward.

CALVERT. Then it's all over bar the voting.

CHRYSTAL. I wish that were true.

CALVERT. If you're running Jago, he can't miss. When the Dean says "jump", we all jump.

CHRYSTAL. Far from it.

CALVERT. Cardinal Chrystal, eminence *grise*. It's nice to be on the winning side.

(CALVERT *exits* L)

BROWN. I like that young man. I'm glad he's for Jago.

CHRYSTAL (*rising and moving to the armchair* LC) Yes. Of course, Jago's not ideal—(*he sits*) but I don't think we'll go far wrong with him.

BROWN. I've only one reservation.

LEWIS. What's that?

BROWN. It's just occurred to me. If Jago becomes Master, who will become Senior Tutor, do you think?

LEWIS. Why, you will, of course.

BROWN. It's not certain.

CHRYSTAL. It's utterly certain, Arthur.

BROWN. Well, then, you see the problem. Am I justified in trying to make Jago Master, when by doing so I may better myself?

LEWIS (*sitting on the armchair* LC) Only a crank could be stopped by such scruples.

BROWN (*with a hoot of laughter*) All right then, Lewis, my conscience is clear. Jago will be a good Master.

LEWIS. I agree.

CHRYSTAL. Let's say he's the best Master we have.

(R.E.A. NIGHTINGALE *enters* L. *He is in his early forties and is suspicious and calculating. He goes to the table up* C *and pours a glass of port for himself*)

Hello, Nightingale. How's the flu?

NIGHTINGALE. I'm recovering—unlike the Master, I gather.

BROWN. The Master has rather more than flu.

NIGHTINGALE. So old Gay has just been telling me. He ran into me in Petty Cury. (*He moves to* R *of Brown*) I thought I'd never get rid of him. You know, it's lamentable to think that when we elect a new Master that old chap will have his vote. He ought to be dis-franchised.

Lewis. If you try to make the College too efficient, Nightingale, you'll suddenly find you've no College at all.

Nightingale. I thought you were a man of advanced opinions, Eliot.

Lewis. Sometimes I am.

Nightingale. Then don't be sentimental. Is anything being done about that, by the way?

Lewis. About what?

Nightingale. The Mastership.

(Chrystal *and* Brown *exchange glances*)

Chrystal (*casually*) People are beginning to mention names.

(Nightingale *crosses above Brown to* r *of Chrystal*)

Brown (*idly*) I think Winslow rather fancies Crawford.

Chrystal (*to Nightingale*) I don't know how *you'd* react to that?

Nightingale. Then I'll tell you. Unenthusiastically.

Brown. That's interesting.

Chrystal. It would be natural if you went for a fellow-scientist.

Nightingale. I might if it weren't Crawford. There's not been a day pass in the last three years when he hasn't reminded me that he's a fellow of the Royal, and that I'm not.

Brown. That's absurd, of course. He's an older man.

Nightingale. He reminds me that I've been up for election six times. This year's my seventh. (*He crosses to the notice-board* l)

Lewis. How do you regard Jago?

Nightingale. Jago? I've got nothing against him.

Chrystal. People will feel there are certain objections. They'll say Jago isn't so distinguished academically as, say, Crawford. And that's a valid point. The only question is, how much weight you give to it.

Brown. Put it another way. Do you prefer Jago, who's respectable on the academic side but not a flyer, or Crawford, who's known to the world at large but who's got other limitations you've just made me see clearly?

Nightingale (*moving to* r *of the desk*) I'm ready to support Jago.

Brown. I value your opinion.

Chrystal. So do I. It'll help me form my own.

Nightingale. I doubt that. You can't pull wool over *my* eyes, Dean. You and Brown are for Jago. It's all settled.

Brown. Then we can count you in for Jago, too?

Nightingale. Yes, why not?

Brown. Good man.

Nightingale. There's just one point.

Brown. Yes.

NIGHTINGALE (*moving below the desk*) How will the College offices go round, once Jago is master?

CHRYSTAL. The only office that can possibly be affected is a tutorship.

BROWN. And tutors are appointed by the Master himself.

NIGHTINGALE. The normal practice is for the Master to ask for advice.

BROWN. Well?

NIGHTINGALE (*turning to Chrystal*) We all know who pulls the strings in this college.

CHRYSTAL. If you're asking me what Jago will do, I assume he'll make Brown Senior Tutor.

LEWIS. That goes without saying.

CHRYSTAL. For the other tutor, he'll have a look round.

NIGHTINGALE (*moving to L of Chrystal*) He'll ask for advice—yours and Brown's.

CHRYSTAL. It's possible.

NIGHTINGALE. It's certain. I want you to know that I expect to be considered. I've been done out of every office in this college since I was elected. I intend to prevent it happening again. (*He moves to the table up C and puts down his glass*)

(BROWN *and* CHRYSTAL *exchange glances*)

BROWN. I'm sure you can be absolutely certain that Jago will consider you very seriously.

NIGHTINGALE. That's too vague.

CHRYSTAL. I'm sorry. We can't be more definite at this stage.

NIGHTINGALE (*moving to R of Chrystal*) It's not good enough, Chrystal.

BROWN. I don't see what more we can possibly do.

NIGHTINGALE. I see what I can do.

CHRYSTAL. What's that?

NIGHTINGALE (*moving to the door L*) Tackle Jago myself.

BROWN. I wouldn't do that just yet, if I were you.

NIGHTINGALE. But you're not, my dear Tutor, you're not.

(NIGHTINGALE *exits L*)

CHRYSTAL. Damn the man! I wish to heaven we could do without him.

BROWN. We can't look a gift-horse in the mouth—even when it's a Nightingale.

CHRYSTAL. No, you're right. (*He rises*) We'd better stop him jumping the gun with Jago. (*He moves to the door L, opens it and calls*) Nightingale—just a moment.

(CHRYSTAL *exits L.* BROWN *rises and moves above the armchair LC to follow Chrystal*)

BROWN (*stopping and turning to Lewis*)　You've never seen a Master elected, have you, Lewis?

LEWIS.　Not yet.

(GETLIFFE *enters* L)

BROWN.　You haven't lived.

(BROWN *turns to go and collides with* GETLIFFE)

GETLIFFE.　Arthur—I'm so sorry.

(BROWN *exits* L)

(*He closes the door*) Ah, Lewis. Look here, what's all this talk about Jago for Master?

LEWIS.　What talk?

GETLIFFE (*moving* C)　Calvert says he's promised his vote and you've promised yours.

LEWIS.　That's right.

GETLIFFE.　Have you gone quite mad?

LEWIS.　I don't think so.

GETLIFFE.　My dear man, we can't have Jago for Master. I don't know what you can be thinking about.

LEWIS.　Jago would make an excellent Master.

GETLIFFE.　Sheer bloody nonsense! What has he done? A book on the Puritan settlers in New England—a commentary on William Bradford's dialogues—he doesn't amount to a row of beans. (*He moves to the table up* C *and picks up the decanter*)

LEWIS.　It's not so much what he's done as what he is. As a human being there's a great deal in him.

GETLIFFE (*pouring a drink*)　Not enough for this job. Not by ten miles.

LEWIS.　The job will make the man.

(*There is a pause.* GETLIFFE *puts down the decanter, picks up his drink and moves to* R *of the armchair* C)

GETLIFFE.　Look—how much are you committed?

LEWIS.　I've made up my mind. Jago satisfies what I want better than anyone else we shall find.

GETLIFFE.　But, good heavens, the man's a ridiculous Tory!

LEWIS.　What of it?

GETLIFFE.　Do you think this is a time to elect Tory figure-heads when there's a chance of a reasonable Radical?

LEWIS.　This job is not a political appointment, Francis.

GETLIFFE.　Every job is a political appointment where men are in the public eye. These days things are balanced so fine we can't afford to give away a single point. You oughtn't to need me to tell you that.

LEWIS.　Whom do you want?

GETLIFFE.　Crawford, of course.

LEWIS. He's conceited. He's shallow. He's a third-rate man.

GETLIFFE. He's one of the best biologists alive. What's more, he's got the right opinions.

LEWIS. You mean, he's got your opinions.

GETLIFFE. And yours.

LEWIS. Politically, yes. I can't take him as a man.

GETLIFFE. There aren't many men of Crawford's standing with radical views who aren't afraid to speak out.

LEWIS. He has no feeling, Francis. (*He rises, moves and puts his newspaper on the table up* R) No glow. And not a scrap of imagination.

GETLIFFE. You claim these things for Jago?

LEWIS. Do you deny them?

GETLIFFE. No. (*He moves below the table up* C) But you forget about the solid virtues. You like humanity for its own sake.

LEWIS. I like imagination rather than ordinariness. (*He moves down* RC) I like self-questioning rather than conceit.

GETLIFFE. Anyway, she is appalling.

LEWIS. She's pathetic. There's much humanity in *her*.

GETLIFFE. She'd be an intolerable nuisance in the Lodge and you know it.

LEWIS. The Lodge could be the making of her. (*He moves to* R *of Getliffe*) In any case, we're not electing her. We're electing her husband.

GETLIFFE. You can't get out of it as though she didn't exist. Crawford's wife knows her place.

LEWIS. Will Crawford be a candidate?

GETLIFFE. If I have anything to do with it. Look, Lewis, be reasonable.

LEWIS. I'm sorry, Francis. This is a job where human beings come first. I want Jago.

GETLIFFE. This is the first time in ten years that you and I have disagreed about anything that mattered.

LEWIS. I don't like it, either.

GETLIFFE. But you're going on with it?

LEWIS. I'm sorry.

GETLIFFE. I warn you, Lewis, if I can find a way to stop this, I shall.

(CALVERT *enters* L)

CALVERT. I've been keeping an eye across the way. No-one's turned up yet and it's just on time.

LEWIS (*moving* RC) Time for what?

CALVERT. Winslow's little convention party. (*He moves to the notice-board*) Haven't you seen the call to arms? (*He reads a notice*) "Those who are not disposed to vote for the Senior Tutor may like to discuss candidates for the Mastership. I suggest a meeting in my rooms at nine-fifteen p.m. on Friday. G. H. W."

(Getliffe *puts his glass on the table up* c)

Not quite the Churchill ring, but we can't have everything.

Lewis. He's being needlessly offensive to Jago.

Calvert (*moving* lc) He can't forgive him for being liked. I wonder how many mugs will show up? It's a quarter past now.

Getliffe (*moving to the door* l; *stiffly*) In that case, you'll excuse me. I don't want to be late.

(Getliffe *exits* l)

Calvert. Calvert in with both feet as usual. (*He moves to the window up* rc) Turn out the lights, old boy. We should get a grandstand view from here.

(Lewis *crosses to the door* l *and switches out the lights.* Calvert *opens the curtains of the windows up* rc *and up* r. Lewis *opens the curtains of the windows up* lc *and up* l. *A pool of light from a lamp in the courtyard illuminates the view outside the windows.* Calvert *and* Lewis *wait in the dark*)

(*After a pause*) Time the enemy appeared.

Lewis (*sitting on the chair* l *of the table up* c) I feel as though I were back at school.

Calvert. So you are. Ah! Mine host in person. Bang on the dot.

(*The church clock strikes the quarter.*
    Winslow *is seen to cross outside the windows from* l *to* r)

You know, he's a damn nuisance, but I like the old stick.

Lewis. So do I.

Calvert (*moving above the left end of the table up* c) Well, he's declared himself, anyway. He'll be sold if he's climbed up a tree for nothing. By the way, I hear Nightingale's in the bag.

Lewis. Yes.

Calvert. God moves in a mysterious way.

(Getliffe *is seen to cross outside the windows from* l *to* r)

Really, Francis ought to know better.

Lewis. He's got some good reasons.

Calvert. He's getting stuffier as he gets older.

(Despard-Smith *is seen to cross outside the windows from* l *to* r)

Hello, here comes Despard.

Lewis. Despard. That's odd. I wonder why.

Calvert. If he weren't able to express a view, it would be nothing short of c-catastrophic.

(Gay *appears outside the windows from* l, *moves* c *and waves to someone off* r)

Lewis. Well, I'm damned! How in God's name did *he* decide?

CALVERT. I don't know, but I bet it was a decision and a half.

(NIGHTINGALE *enters outside the windows from* R *and crosses to* GAY. *They talk for a moment*)

Hello. Judas?

(LEWIS *rises and stands* L *of* CALVERT. *They watch.*
NIGHTINGALE *is seen to shake his head, then he crosses and exits* L.
GAY *exits* R)

LEWIS (*with relief*) Apparently not.
CALVERT. I wonder if old Winslow is still hoping. I wonder if he expects to be asked to stand himself.
LEWIS. People hope on, long after they admit it to themselves.
CALVERT. Of course, he hasn't a prayer. (*Suddenly*) Ah! "Here comes the bride." Ta-rum-ta-tum!

(CRAWFORD *is seen to cross outside the windows from* L *to* R)

(*He crosses to* R *of the table up* C) What do you think his chances are?
LEWIS. If they ask him to stand, he may not accept.
CALVERT. If Crawford's asked, he'll accept all right.

(*There is a pause.* LEWIS *and* CALVERT *look at each other, then* LEWIS *goes to the window up* LC, *opens it and looks out.* CALVERT *goes to the window up* RC, *opens it and looks out*)

LEWIS. I believe that's the lot.
CALVERT. If it is, we're home and dry.

(*There is a pause.* LEWIS *and* CALVERT *look at each other, then out of the windows again*)

(*After a pause*) It is, you know. It's in the bag!

(CALVERT *and* LEWIS *close their respective windows.*
CHRYSTAL *and* BROWN *enter suddenly* L. BROWN *switches on the lights*)

BROWN. What happened? A fuse?
CALVERT. No. A power failure. The opposition's down the drain.
CHRYSTAL (*moving to* L *of the table up* C; *sharply*) What's that?
CALVERT (*moving to* R *of the table up* C) Winslow only got five takers.
CHRYSTAL. Five. Are you sure?
CALVERT (*moving to the chair above the chess-table*) Only five went into the tunnel of love. (*He turns the chair to face* L *and sits*)
CHRYSTAL. Which five?
LEWIS (*crossing above the table up* C *to* R *of it*) Getliffe, Crawford, Despard, Gay and Winslow himself.

(BROWN *moves down* LC)

CHRYSTAL (*moving* C) That's all?

Calvert. The lot.
Brown. They've lost face.
Chrystal. Yes.
Calvert (*happily*) The frost is on the pumpkin, gentlemen.
Brown (*moving to L of the armchair LC*) All the same, I'm sorry about Gay. They've stolen a march on us there.
Lewis (*moving above the armchair RC*) Still, it's pretty good.
Brown. I must say it looks perfectly splendid. (*He crosses to L of Lewis*) Mind you, Lewis, we mustn't throw our hats in the air. If we let them feel we think it's safe . . .
Calvert. Arthur, you're the only man in the world who treats Lewis like an irresponsible schoolboy. It gives me great pleasure.

(Luke *enters abruptly* L. Brown *and* Chrystal *turn to him*)

Luke. What's this? A reply to Winslow's meeting?
Lewis. Roughly.
Luke (*moving LC*) What do you mean "roughly"? It's a meeting of Jago's supporters, isn't it?
Brown. One or two of us have come to the conclusion that Jago's the right man.
Luke. So have I.

(Calvert *rises*)

So why wasn't I asked to this bloody caucus?
Chrystal. To be frank, Luke, we thought that as a fellow-scientist you would naturally vote for Crawford.
Luke. I'm damned if I vote for Crawford. What am I—a bloody fool? All right, as a boffin he may have a brain like a rocket but the rest of him's knee-high to a gnat.

(Brown *moves below the right end of the table up* C)

Chrystal. Luke, you're not yet a permanency here. You'll have to look to Crawford and Getliffe to make a case for you if the college is going to keep you.
Luke. I know all that . . .
Lewis. Francis Getliffe's a fair-minded man.
Chrystal (*moving to R of the armchair* C) Just the same, none of us will blame Luke if he avoids risking his future.
Luke (*moving above the armchair* C) The hell with that! We're electing a Master and Jago stands out a mile. Anyone who doubts it should spend an hour with him. He'll make one of the best Masters this or any other college——

(Jago *enters unnoticed* L)

—has ever had, will Jago, and I'm damned if I'll vote for anyone else.
Jago (*moving LC*) It's extremely good of you to say so, Luke——

(LUKE *moves* R)

—but I think perhaps I ought to remind you that so far I've not been officially invited to stand.

CHRYSTAL (*moving to* R *of Jago; briskly*) That's easily settled. Jago, are you prepared to stand for the Mastership? Because if so, I think it's yours.

JAGO. I'm all attention.

CHRYSTAL. As you know, the college has thirteen fellows, not counting the present Master. (*He moves* C) I can promise you the votes of all five of us here in this room, plus Pilbrow and Nightingale. And that gets you home.

JAGO. Nightingale! I'm astonished!

BROWN. Yes, we were a little surprised ourselves.

JAGO (*moving to* R *of the desk*) And dear old Eustace Pilbrow. I don't suppose we've agreed on a single public issue since I became a Fellow. Yet he's willing to do this for me?

BROWN. He's very fond of you personally, Paul.

JAGO. Wonderful. I'm deeply touched.

BROWN (*moving down* C) And I'm sure you're heartened by Roy's support—and Lewis's and Luke's.

JAGO. Indeed I am. But I've always been better with young men than with people my own age. I don't have to show off to them, you see.

CHRYSTAL. There it is, then, Jago. That's your majority.

BROWN. Of course, the picture could just conceivably change before things happen to the present Master as they must.

LUKE (*bluntly*) I shan't change.

CALVERT. Nor I.

LEWIS. We've made up our minds.

CHRYSTAL. In that case, you can count on us to put you in the Lodge—if that's what you want.

BROWN. Is that what you want, Paul?

JAGO (*after a pause*) Gentlemen, I—I feel that my feet aren't quite firm under me. Since it became a possibility that I might be asked, I've had several sleepless nights about this, asking myself whether I ought to do it, whether I wanted to do it, whether I could do it. There's one thing I've become convinced of, even in the small hours—you know, when one's whole life seems completely pointless. (*He moves below the armchair* LC, *turns and faces the others*) I'm going to tell you now, without modesty, between friends—I think I can do it. I think I can do it better than anyone within reach—so—if you want me—yes, I'll stand.

BROWN. Splendid!

LUKE. Good man!

CHRYSTAL (*crossing to* L *of the armchair* LC) I'm glad to hear it, Jago.

CALVERT. This calls for a bottle.

Brown. Yes, indeed.

(*They all move to the table up* c. Chrystal *and* Luke *stand above the table.* Lewis *moves to* l *of the table and pours the wine.* Jago *stands below the left end of the table,* Calvert *below the centre of the table and* Brown *stands* l *of Jago*)

Jago. Oh, my friends—I'm so grateful to you all. I wish it were easier to say how much. One risks making an ass of oneself on these occasions. I love this place, every stick and stone of it. I'd like to do something for it; I want to leave some sort of mark. Forgive me if I'm rather overwhelmed by the thought that one day I may be able to say, "This is my College."

(*They all take a glass*)

Calvert (*raising his glass*) Gentlemen; our next Master, Dr Paul Jago!
Omnes. Our next master, Dr Paul Jago!

(*They drink.*
     Crawford *is seen to cross outside the windows from* r *to* l)

Jago. Thank you. Thank you—from my heart.

(Brown *sits on the centre chair below the table up* c. Calvert *sits* r *of Brown.* Chrystal *sits on the centre chair above the table.* Lewis *sits* l *of Chrystal.* Luke *stands between Chrystal and Lewis*)

(*He moves in to* l *of the table*) Oh, I know I can—we can—make this a fine college—a great college. That's why I'm so glad we've got you younger men with us. We'll need money, of course, but from what I hear, Dean, you and the tutor have not been idle in that direction.
Lewis. No, indeed.
Jago. Splendid! That's splendid! I truly believe that with your support——

(Crawford *enters* l)

—I shall be able to say before long . . . (*He sees Crawford and breaks off*)
Crawford (*easily*) Ah, Jago. I was about to send you a note but now that won't be necesssary. I think you ought to know I've just been asked to let myself be a candidate for the Mastership. Those who asked me to stand are not a majority of the Fellows, but they represent a sound body of opinion. I don't approve of people who have to be persuaded to play, like the young woman who just happens to have brought her music. So I told them I was ready to let my name go forward.
Jago (*after a moment*) I'm very grateful to you for telling me.
Crawford. It was the least I could do. After all, you and I are bound to be the only serious candidates.

c

JAGO (*gracefully*) I wish both the candidates reached the standard of distinction set by one of them.

CRAWFORD. Thank you, Jago. I just wanted to be sure you knew the position. Good night to you all.

(*All but* JAGO *murmur* "*Good night*".
CRAWFORD *exits* L. *There is a moment's silence*)

JAGO (*picking up his glass*) I'd give a lot for his assurance.

CALVERT. I've never thought of you as lacking assurance, Jago.

JAGO. Haven't you, Roy? (*With a sudden surge of confidence*) Tell me something, would Crawford make a good Master?

CHRYSTAL. No.

LEWIS. Crawford? Never.

CALVERT. Good God, no!

BROWN. You're our man, Paul.

(LEWIS *rises*.
CRAWFORD *is seen to cross outside the windows from* L *to* R)

LUKE (*moving to* R *of Jago*) To hell with Crawford! Jago for Master.

JAGO (*with a broad smile*) Am I tempting fate if I drink to that myself?

JAGO *raises his glass as—*

the CURTAIN *falls*

To face page 29——_The Masters, Act II_   _Photo by Houston Rogers_

ACT II

SCENE I

SCENE—*The Garden of the Master's Lodge. Three weeks later. Night.*
The Lodge is L *with a door leading into the drawing-room. Up* RC *is an oak tree and a panoramic view of the river and college buildings. A buffet-table set with a white cloth and a bowl of punch is* LC. *A small round table is* RC *with garden chairs above and* R *of it. There are two chairs side by side up* L *and other chairs stand down* R, *down* C *and down* L. *A garden seat is* R *of the oak tree, facing up* L.

When the CURTAIN *rises it is a fine, moonlit summer night, Cambridge at its loveliest. The lights are on in the Lodge. The stage is empty.* MRS MURIEL ROYCE *enters from the Lodge, carrying a tray of glasses.* JOAN ROYCE, *her daughter, enters* R, *carrying two small cushions. She is aged twenty.* MRS ROYCE *puts the tray of glasses on the table)*

JOAN (*putting the cushions on the chairs at the table* RC) There must be mice in the shed. They've been eating the cushions.

MRS ROYCE (L *of the table* LC; *surveying the glasses*) Now I wonder if that's enough.

JOAN (*crossing to* R *of the table* LC) Plenty.

MRS ROYCE. Some of them always prefer the drawing-room, but one can never be sure how many.

(CALVERT *enters from the Lodge, carrying a deck-chair. He wears evening dress and tails)*

CALVERT. Where shall I put it?

MRS ROYCE. Oh, thank you, Roy. (*She indicates*) Over here, I think.

(CALVERT *sets up the deck-chair down* L *of the table* LC)

JOAN. Who's it for?

MRS ROYCE. Professor Gay—he always likes that chair. Your father was particularly anxious that we shouldn't forget it.

CALVERT. Are you sure the Master won't mind us all coming here tonight?

MRS ROYCE. On the contrary, he'd be most upset if you didn't. Both he and I want everything to be as bright and cheerful as it always is after a feast. Now—cigars—Roy, you'll find them somewhere in the Master's study.

JOAN (*crossing to the Lodge*) I know where they are. In the third drawer.

(CALVERT *and* JOAN *exit to the Lodge.* MRS ROYCE *moves to the door.*

ALICE JAGO *enters up* L. *She is a plain, physically graceless woman, never sure of herself for an instant, but determined not to be overlooked. She carries a bunch of flowers)*

MRS ROYCE (*calling into the Lodge*) Joan, some ashtrays.
JOAN (*off*) Right.

(MRS ROYCE *turns and sees Alice*)

MRS ROYCE. Mrs Jago!
ALICE (*moving* C) I'm afraid I startled you.
MRS ROYCE. Yes, a little.
ALICE (*at once; defensively*) You don't have to tell me I shouldn't be here, Mrs Royce; I know tonight is just for the men—but they won't be out from the feast for another ten minutes. I asked. That's why I came this way. I shouldn't have. I can see I've embarrassed you.
MRS ROYCE (*moving below the table* LC) Not in the least.
ALICE. I wouldn't have dreamt of coming, but Paul has rather a lot on his mind just now, and he forgot these. (*She indicates the flowers*) Oh, dear, they're beginning to wilt already. Once cut, they die so quickly, don't they? (*She moves to* R *of Mrs Royce and hands her the flowers*) For the Master.
MRS ROYCE. How very kind.
ALICE (*moving* C) Paul asked me to pick them specially.
MRS ROYCE (*putting the flowers on the table* LC) The Master will be most touched. (*She moves* L)
ALICE. You won't tell Paul I had to bring them? He'd be upset to realize he'd forgotten.
MRS ROYCE. Of course I won't, if you don't wish it.
ALICE. Thank you.

(*There is an awkward silence*)

(*She moves to* R *of the table* LC) Is that the traditional brandy punch?
MRS ROYCE. Yes. (*She moves up* L *of the table* LC) Would you care for a glass?
ALICE (*moving* C) Oh, no. Thank you.
MRS ROYCE. This bowl was one of our wedding presents—the Master's and mine—from Gordon Ellerman—he became Master of Peterhouse, you know.
ALICE. Really?

(*There is another awkward silence*)

MRS ROYCE. Perhaps you'd like to come in for a moment?
ALICE. That's very kind of you, but—no, I won't actually come in, but perhaps I might—I wonder—could I take a quick look at your drawing-room? (*She crosses to the Lodge door*)
MRS ROYCE (*taken aback*) Yes, of course. (*She moves down* LC)
ALICE (*eagerly*) It would be so helpful. You see, I've rather forgotten . . . (*She looks in the downstage windows*) Oh, yes; I'm afraid our

furniture isn't quite like yours. And all those curtains. There's such a lot to plan, isn't there? (*She turns*) I do so want Paul to be proud of his Lodge. Oh—forgive me!

Mrs Royce. Please. I know that my husband's probable successor will be Dr Jago.

Alice (*at once*) It's quite certain.

Mrs Royce. I'm glad.

Alice (*moving to* l *of Mrs Royce*) Are you? Yes, of course you are. Everyone is. Tell me, how is the Master?

Mrs Royce. There's no change. There can't be.

Alice. I'm so very sorry.

Mrs Royce. Thank you.

Alice. You take it so calmly. If it were Paul, I . . . You don't know my husband really well, do you, Mrs Royce?

Mrs Royce. Not very well. We've met many times, of course.

Alice. He's such a great man, you know. I'm afraid I'm a dreadful burden to him.

Mrs Royce. Oh, I'm sure not.

Alice. I can see by your face that you don't really mean that.

Mrs Royce. My dear Mrs Jago . . .

Alice. I shall have to learn the polite lie myself, shan't I? All the social graces. (*She crosses above the chair* c *to* r *of the table* lc) I must go. You won't forget the flowers?

Mrs Royce (*moving down* l *of the table* lc) No.

Alice. They're from Paul. You will remember.

Mrs Royce. I will. Good night, Mrs Jago—and thank you.

Alice. It was nothing. Nothing at all. (*She turns and moves* r *to go, but stops suddenly and returns to* c) Mrs Royce, I'm going to say something you won't like. I can't help it. (*With devastating candour*) You shouldn't lie to your husband about his death. It's wickedly wrong. Don't tell me to mind my own business. It's too important for that. I'm sure you mean well, ·but meaning isn't enough. No-one knows that better than I. You see . . . .

Mrs Royce (*quietly*) It was kind of you to bring the flowers. Good night.

Alice (*contrite*) I'm sorry. I—(*helplessly*) I'm sorry.

(Alice *turns and stumbles out* r. Mrs Royce *leans on the table* lc, *her eyes closed*)

Calvert (*off* l) Didn't you know? I'm riddled with vices.

Joan (*off* l) But smoking cigars isn't one of them?

Calvert (*off* l) Smoking cigars isn't one of them.

(Calvert *and* Joan *enter from the Lodge.* Calvert *carries a box of cigars.* Joan *carries two ashtrays and a table-lighter*)

(*He moves up* l *of the table* lc *and puts the box on it*) Corona-Coronas! Old Gay'll be delighted when he sees these.

(JOAN *crosses and puts an ashtray and the lighter on the table* RC. *The sound of a choir singing is heard in the distance.*

MRS ROYCE *picks up the flowers and exits to the Lodge, without a word.* CALVERT *looks after her.* JOAN *crosses to the table* LC *and puts the ashtray on it, then moves up* RC *and looks off up* R)

JOAN (*listening*) They're practising at King's.
CALVERT. Yes.

(JOAN *turns down* RC *and buries her face in her hands.* CALVERT *crosses above the table* LC *to* L *of Joan and takes her shoulders*)

JOAN (*thinking of her father*) Just to be alive—to be living—that's enough, isn't it, on a night like this?
CALVERT (*gently*) Have some brandy punch. (*He crosses to the table* LC *and fills two glasses*)
JOAN. No, thanks.
CALVERT. Come on, you're looking particularly fetching to-night.
JOAN (*crossing to him*) Am I? All right.

(CALVERT *hands a glass to Joan*)

Our last feast. I wonder who'll live in the Lodge after father. Jago or Crawford?
CALVERT. The betting's on Jago—seven to four.
JOAN. You want Jago, don't you?
CALVERT. Yes, I want Jago.
JOAN. Then I hope it's Jago—Crawford's a cold fish.
CALVERT (*raising his glass*) *Skol!*
JOAN (*raising her glass*) *Skol!*

(*They drink. The sound of the singing fades*)

CALVERT. You know, arteries harden and hair falls out but your mother's punch gets stronger every year.
JOAN (*moving* RC) Roy, you will go on working on father's manuscripts, won't you?
CALVERT. If I'm asked.
JOAN. He wouldn't want anyone else. Do you know, he says you're the most remarkable scholar this College has produced for fifty years.
CALVERT (*moving down* R *of the table* LC) Good Lord, did he really say that?
JOAN. Thank heavens you don't look it.

(*They laugh.*
MRS ROYCE *enters from the Lodge*)

MRS ROYCE (*moving* LC) Roy, I've forgotten to uncork the claret and I know Mr Winslow always prefers it.

Calvert (*putting his glass on the table* lc) Coming.

(Calvert *exits to the Lodge.* Joan *crosses below the table* lc *to* l *of it*)

Mrs Royce (*moving towards the Lodge*) I don't know why but I'm always an idiot with a corkscrew.

(Jago *enters up* l *and crosses above the table* lc *to* r *of it. Like all the dons in this Act, he wears white tie and tails*)

Jago (*to Joan*) Hello, my dear.
Joan. Dr Jago.
Mrs Royce (*turning and crossing to* r *of the chair* c) Senior Tutor—how good of you to come. Such a beautiful evening.
Jago. Cambridge is unbeatable on a night like this. You can smell the acacia and the lilac. How is the Master?
Mrs Royce. There's no great change. (*She moves to* l *of Jago and turns to the table*) Now, what can we offer you? This, of course, is brandy punch, or there's port and claret in the drawing-room.
Jago. Punch, thank you.

(Joan *moves to* l *of the table, puts down her glass and pours a glass of punch for Jago*)

But are you positive you want us tonight? I can easily discourage the others.
Mrs Royce. No, no. I wouldn't hear of it. It's a tradition of centuries that the fellows take wine at the Lodge after the Commemoration of Benefactors. We wouldn't consider breaking it. Besides, the master might suspect, and I won't have that. Of course, it's not easy for us, but it's best for him, and that's what matters. (*She hands Jago his drink*) Now, if you'll excuse me—and do please make yourself at home, won't you, Dr Jago?

(Mrs Royce *exits to the Lodge*)

Joan. I'm glad it's you who will be following father here.
Jago. My dear child . . .
Joan (*crossing above the table to* l *of Jago*) Oh, you don't have to avoid the subject. If father knew, it's the last thing he'd want. He'd be completely detached about himself, and absolutely fascinated about the succession. That's why I'm sure mother's making a mistake. I mean, we shouldn't hold back anything vital. We're not wise enough to know.
Jago. That's a curious remark from a girl your age. When I was twenty, I was certain I knew everything.
Joan. You're a man. Men grow up late.
Jago (*with a broad smile*) Very late.

(Gay *and* Despard-Smith *enter up* l. Gay *wears an incredibly old set of tails and some obscure medals from the Boer War.* Despard-Smith *is still in his clerical collar*)

GAY (*as he enters*) Ah. That was a capital feast. That was a feast and a half and no mistake. (*He moves to* L *of Joan*) Good evening, my dear.

JOAN. Professor.

(DESPARD-SMITH *stands up* L *of the table* LC)

GAY. I particularly enjoyed the asparagus. You never did relish asparagus, did you, Despard?

DESPARD-SMITH (*gloomily*) It d-disagrees with me.

GAY. That weak tummy of yours. You want to watch it. Old men's tum-tums can be troublesome. Ah, do I see my deck-chair? Capital! (*He moves to the deck-chair and sits*)

(JOAN *moves to the table* LC, *fills a glass with punch and hands it to Despard-Smith.* JAGO *moves up* R)

I remember having some particularly succulent asparagus in Oxford one night when they happened to be giving me an honorary degree. Do you know, that asparagus slipped down just as though it was taking part in the celebration.

(WINSLOW *enters up* L *and stands above the table* LC)

Ah, Winslow, what a magnificent feast this has been.

WINSLOW. Are you going to congratulate *me* on it?

GAY. Certainly not.

(WINSLOW *moves to* L *of the table.* JOAN *fills a glass with punch for Gay*)

You gave up being steward a great number of years ago. I shall congratulate the man responsible for this excellent feast. Young Getliffe is our present steward.

(JOAN *picks up the drink and moves up* L *of Gay*)

Where is young Getliffe? I congratulate him. Splendid work these young scientists do. (*To Joan*) Now, what have we here?

JOAN (*handing Gay the glass*) Brandy punch.

GAY. Brandy punch? That's a drink and a half!

(JOAN *joins Winslow and Despard-Smith.*
CRAWFORD, GETLIFFE, LEWIS *and* NIGHTINGALE *enter up* L. CRAWFORD *wears a C.B.E. cross,* NIGHTINGALE *a D.S.O., M.C., and Bar. They group up* RC. LEWIS *is* L *of the group,* GETLIFFE *is* R *of Lewis,* CRAWFORD *is* R *of Getliffe and* NIGHTINGALE *is* R *of Crawford.* CRAWFORD *is smoking a cigar*)

CRAWFORD (*as they enter*) Of course, I was flattered to be asked to sit on the committee, but, you know, selecting people for honorific purposes, though an interesting job, is not as easy as you might suppose.

GETLIFFE. Which purposes are you referring to?

CRAWFORD. I was thinking of the choice of Fellows of the Royal,

which I happen just to have been concerned with. Speaking as a
man of science, I should be happier if there were sharper criteria to
help make the choice.

LEWIS. "Original work of distinction"—isn't that the yardstick?

CRAWFORD. Yes, but how can you compare one man with a new
theory on the interior of the stars, with someone else who has pain-
stakingly measured the movements of a fish?

(NIGHTINGALE *moves to* R *of the table* RC. CRAWFORD *moves to* L
of the table RC, *and taps the ash from his cigar into the ashtray.*

CALVERT *enters from the Lodge, collects the box of cigars and a box
of matches from the table* LC *and moves to* L *of* GAY *who takes a cigar.*
CALVERT *lights it for him.* JOAN *moves to* R *of the table* LC, *pours two
glasses of punch and hands them to Lewis and Getliffe*)

NIGHTINGALE. By the way, Crawford, speaking of the Royal
Society, do you happen to know when the results will be out?

CRAWFORD. The council will make its recommendations on
Thursday. Of course, they're not public for a couple of months
after. Is there anyone you're interested in?

NIGHTINGALE (*intensely*) Yes.

CRAWFORD. You're not up yourself, are you?

NIGHTINGALE. Yes, I am.

CRAWFORD. I'm afraid I didn't realize it. Of course, your subject
is a long way from mine. I don't think I've heard anything about
the chemists' lists. We must see what we can do. (*He turns away to the
table* LC) Now, who's going to give me some brandy punch?

(JOAN *fills a glass for Crawford then sits in the chair* C)

NIGHTINGALE (*turning to Jago*) Er—Jago . . .

JAGO (*moving to* L *of Nightingale*) Hello, Nightingale. Look at that
lilac. Isn't it perfect?

NIGHTINGALE. Jago, about the future of the college—I imagine
you've been giving some thought to it lately.

(JAGO *and* NIGHTINGALE *move down* R. CALVERT *goes to the table*
LC, *replaces the cigars and matches and fills a glass of punch for himself*)

JAGO. My dear man, I've been thinking of little else.

NIGHTINGALE. Good. Then you'll have a clear idea of who you'll
want for the tutorship.

JAGO. Oh, no. No, I've been thinking in general terms. No, something as vital as a tutorship requires the most detailed consideration.
There are so many factors to be considered.

NIGHTINGALE. Such as?

JAGO. I would put first a disinterested love of the job. Then
academic distinction, popularity with one's colleagues . . .

(NIGHTINGALE *and* JAGO *move up* R, *talking together.* WINSLOW *and*
DESPARD-SMITH *move up* C. CRAWFORD *joins* DESPARD-SMITH *and*

WINSLOW *and they group* L *of the tree.* GETLIFFE *and* LEWIS *move up* L *of the table* LC. CALVERT *puts his glass on the table* LC *and moves to* R *of* JOAN *who is lost in her thoughts*)

CALVERT (*to Joan*) Come on the river and I'll tell you tales of Babylon and Tyre.
JOAN. Did you say on it, or in it?
CALVERT. Both, if you like.
JOAN. I ought to stay here and cope.
CALVERT. You're not coping. You're just part of the decorations.
JOAN (*rising*) Well, we mustn't be long.
CALVERT (*putting an arm around her*) We won't be. Come on.

(CALVERT *and* JOAN *cross and exit up* R. JAGO *and* NIGHTINGALE, *deep in conversation, move to* R *of the table* RC)

NIGHTINGALE (*urgently*) But I must know where I stand, Jago.
JAGO. I'm sorry. I really can't say more at this stage. No, that would be quite unethical, Nightingale. Quite wrong. But I can say that, when the time comes to settle the tutorship, your name will be considered, along with the rest, with the utmost care.
NIGHTINGALE (*curtly*) Thank you, Jago. (*He turns away up* R)

(BROWN, CHRYSTAL *and* SIR HORACE TIMBERLAKE *enter up* L. SIR HORACE *is a well-kept, well-washed, well-fed figure. He is smoking a cigar*)

BROWN (*as they enter*) This way, Sir Horace.

(SIR HORACE *moves to* R *of the table* LC. BROWN *stands* R *of Sir Horace.* CHRYSTAL *moves to* L *of the table* LC)

SIR HORACE. Thank you. Ah, how peaceful it all is. The trees and the river—the quietness and the calm. You don't realize, gentlemen, what a temptation it would be to quit the rough-and-tumble and settle down here.
CHRYSTAL. I'll change with you, Sir Horace.
BROWN. The dean has always admired industrial power.
SIR HORACE. You wouldn't get such peace, Mr Chrystal.
CHRYSTAL. Are some of your colleagues on speaking terms? Ours just manage it.
BROWN (*crossing above Sir Horace to the table* LC) Punch, sir?
SIR HORACE. Thank you.

(BROWN *fills a glass of punch for Sir Horace.* WINSLOW *and* DESPARD-SMITH *move to* R *of Sir Horace.* CRAWFORD *sits on the garden seat up* RC. NIGHTINGALE *moves and stands behind Crawford*)

(*He turns to Despard-Smith*) That chapel of yours, Padre—now that's very fine. A splendid piece of eighteenth-century panelling you've got.

(CHRYSTAL *moves up* R *of Gay*)

(*To Winslow*) I suppose it must be eighteenth-century, mustn't it, Bursar?

WINSLOW. I'm sure you're right, Sir Horace. (*He sits on the chair above the table* RC) But you're bound to be better informed than I. I've not been inside the building for thirty years.
SIR HORACE (*moving down* C) Indeed, sir.

(DESPARD-SMITH *moves to* R *of Sir Horace*)

You don't know what you've missed.
BROWN (*taking the drink to Sir Horace*) Punch, Sir Horace?
SIR HORACE (*taking the glass*) Thank you.

(BROWN *moves a little up* C. LEWIS *moves to* R *of Chrystal*)

LEWIS (*to Chrystal; sotto voce*) Any sign of the cheque-book?
CHRYSTAL (*sotto voce*) Not yet, but we're hoping.

(LEWIS *rejoins Getliffe up* L)

SIR HORACE (*to Despard-Smith*) I was very much impressed by your Commemoration Service. There was nothing showy about it —you know what I mean.
DESPARD-SMITH. I'm glad we p-pleased you.
GAY. Yes, a splendid service. I particularly enjoyed the lesson. "Let us now praise famous men." We hear slightly too much nowadays about praising the obscure. Very fine people in their way, but they shouldn't get all the hallelujahs. (*To Sir Horace*) Do you mind telling me your name?
SIR HORACE. I'm Timberlake.
GAY. Have you any connection with the College?
SIR HORACE. My nephew is an undergraduate.
GAY. I congratulate you.
SIR HORACE. I'm proud the boy's a part of it here. This college has a kind of historical magic. You know what I mean, Dr Jago?
JAGO (*with great warmth; this is his subject*) You can trace each step —in the muniment-room, in the chapel, the library, the Lodge. Do you know, sir, the bottles of wine drunk by each fellow are on record, back almost for two hundred years?
SIR HORACE (*crossing to* L *of the table* RC) Is that so?

(DESPARD-SMITH *moves up* C)

CHRYSTAL. A chair, Sir Horace? (*He moves the chair* C *to* L *of the table* RC)

(MRS ROYCE *enters from the Lodge*)

MRS ROYCE (*crossing to* C) Good evening, gentlemen.

(WINSLOW *and* CRAWFORD *rise.* SIR HORACE, *about to sit, straightens up.* BROWN *moves up* L *of Sir Horace.* CHRYSTAL *steps back to the down*

L *corner of the table* LC. WINSLOW *moves* R *of the table* RC. LEWIS *and*
GETLIFFE *move to* L *of the table* LC)

BROWN. Mrs Royce, may I present our guest—Sir Horace
Timberlake? (*He moves a little up* RC)

(CRAWFORD *and* NIGHTINGALE *move up* C)

MRS ROYCE (*shaking hands with Timberlake*) How do you do, Sir
Horace? I'm so sorry my husband isn't here to receive you, but he's
confined to bed with a duodenal.
SIR HORACE. I know those fellows. Milk and slops, little and often.
My best wishes to him for a speedy recovery.
MRS ROYCE. Thank you. (*She looks around*) Now, is everyone here?
I don't see Mr Pilbrow.
BROWN. Pilbrow's abroad, and Luke is working late at the
Cavendish. Otherwise, this is the college.
MRS ROYCE. Well, gentlemen, my husband wishes me to tell you
how sorry he is that he can't welcome you himself, but he's particu-
larly anxious that you should carry on just as usual. And there's no
need to whisper and hush. I assure you, you can't possibly disturb
him from here. (*She turns and crosses to* R *of Gay*) Now, if it gets too
chilly, there's a fire indoors. And if anyone prefers it, there's port
and claret in the drawing-room. Mr Winslow, you're a claret man,
I think.
WINSLOW (*crossing to* C) I am indeed, ma'am. I am indeed.
MRS ROYCE. I always feel on these occasions that I should apologize for being an unregenerate teetotaller. (*She crosses to the Lodge*)
WINSLOW (*following Mrs Royce*) On the contrary, you correct the
balance.

(MRS ROYCE *and* WINSLOW *exit to the Lodge.*
    GETLIFFE, NIGHTINGALE *and* CRAWFORD *follow them off.*
CHRYSTAL *moves to* R *of the table* LC. BROWN *moves above the table* RC.
SIR HORACE *sits* L *of the table* RC. JAGO *sits above the table* RC.
DESPARD-SMITH *moves* C *and is attacked by a bout of coughing*)

GAY (*to Despard-Smith*) Catching cold?
DESPARD-SMITH. Certainly not.
GAY. You want to watch that chest of yours.
DESPARD-SMITH. There's nothing wrong with my chest. (*He moves
to the Lodge*) It's the wallflowers. I'm allergic to w-w-wallflowers.

(DESPARD-SMITH *exits wheezing to the Lodge*)

GAY (*happily*) He'll be the next.

(CHRYSTAL *moves up* L *of Sir Horace.* LEWIS *perches on the upstage
end of the table* LC. BROWN *sits above the table* RC)

SIR HORACE. You know, the atmosphere of this place is absorbing
to an outsider. There's something quite magnificent about it. You
know what I mean?

Jago. And yet we began in the humblest way, as a kind of medieval boarding-house.

Sir Horace. A boarding-house?

Jago. Yes. You see, the first undergraduates who came up to Cambridge . . .

Chrystal. Get Jago on his hobby-horse and he won't draw breath till morning, Sir Horace. (*He moves to* R *of the table* LC *and helps himself to punch*)

Sir Horace. Go on, Dr Jago, I'm fascinated.

Jago. Well, the first undergraduates lived in the town and looked after themselves and did what they chose. One can picture them reeling hilariously through the streets, full of the wild hopes of youth. And so the boarding-house appeared, to keep the young men out of mischief, and this college of ours was founded, towards the end of the fourteenth-century, by taking over a simple rooming-house. It was poor, unpretentious, it counted for little. But it had a Master, it had eight fellow-scholars—and it had the same first court as now. It gives one a glow to think that if a fourteenth-century member of the college were to be dropped in our first court today, he would be instantaneously at home.

Sir Horace. You're a romantic, Dr Jago. You love this place.

Jago. Yes, I do.

Sir Horace. I suppose the world is as unstable tonight as it's ever been in human experience——

(Chrystal *moves up* L *of Sir Horace*)

—but it's impossible to believe that, sitting here in a Cambridge garden, enjoying your hospitality.

(Chrystal *crosses to the chair down* L *and moves it down* L *of Sir Horace*)

And, by the by, speaking of hospitality, at that little dinner you gave me last term, I seem to remember we had some conversation about the financial position of the college.

Brown (*sitting forward; alert*) Yes, Sir Horace?

Sir Horace. Well, now . . .

(Winslow *enters from the Lodge, carrying a glass of claret.* Chrystal *sees Winslow and clears his throat loudly*)

Chrystal (*quickly*) Let me fill your glass, Sir Horace. (*He takes Sir Horace's glass, crosses to the table* LC, *signals to Lewis to get Winslow out of the way, then refills Sir Horace's glass*)

Lewis (*rising and moving down* LC) I think I'll take a stroll by the water. Care to join me, Bursar?

Winslow (*taking in the group* R) I don't mind in the least being got rid of—(*he puts his glass on the downstage end of the table* LC) but I confess to a weakness for wanting to know why.

(Lewis *and* Winslow *move up* R *together*)

Lewis. How did your son get on in the Tripos?

Winslow. My dear Eliot, I can't answer for the prospects of the semi-illiterate. I can only hope the wretched boy managed to read the questions.

(Lewis *and* Winslow *exit up* r)

Chrystal (*crossing and handing Sir Horace his drink*) I must apologize for the Bursar. He's one of our liabilities.

Sir Horace. Every organization has its difficult men.

Brown. Now, Sir Horace, I believe you were about to say . . .

Sir Horace (*indicating the oak*) That's a fine old tree.

Brown. What?

Sir Horace. A really splendid tree, that.

Chrystal. Magnificent, isn't it?

Sir Horace. Solid. Enduring. Like your college, Dr Jago.

Chrystal (*sitting in the chair* l *of Sir Horace*) Of course, to endure today, one must also expand.

Brown (*to Sir Horace*) And speaking of expansion, when the bursar came out I believe he interrupted your train of thought.

Sir Horace. Did he? What was I saying?

Brown. You were good enough to refer to the last time we met when the topic of conversation . . .

Sir Horace. Ah, yes. I think someone suggested that for certain lines of development the College might need a little help. I think you suggested that, Mr Chrystal.

Chrystal. I did.

Sir Horace. I think you also said that you needed financial help with no conditions attached to it.

Brown. I believe the dean did vaguely indicate something of the sort—or are we misremembering, Dean?

Chrystal. No, you're perfectly right.

Sir Horace (*putting his glass on the table in front of him*) Well, I've been turning it over in my mind.

Chrystal. Yes, Sir Horace.

Sir Horace. I dare say you've thought about it more deeply than I have, but I can't help feeling that some people wouldn't be prepared to exert themselves for you on those terms. You know what I mean? Some people might be inclined to see if financial help could be forthcoming, but would be put off at just making it over to you for general purposes. You take my point, Dr Jago?

Jago. I'm sure we should all agree that it would be foolish only to accept money for general purposes, but you know we've suffered quite an amount from benefactions which are tied down so much that we can't really use them. For instance, we've got the income on twenty thousand pounds for scholarships for the sons of Protestant clergymen in Galway. That's really rather tantalizing.

Sir Horace. I see that. But let me put a point of view some people might take. Some people might fancy that institutions like this are always tempted to put too much capital into bricks and mortar.

JAGO. It's the go-ahead colleges who are building.

SIR HORACE. I'm afraid I don't agree with you. If people of my way of thinking got together some financial help, I'm inclined to think it would be for men.

CHRYSTAL. Men?

JAGO. Men?

SIR HORACE. Yes. This country is short of first-class men.

JAGO. All countries are short of first-class men, Sir Horace.

SIR HORACE. But some are shorter than others. We want to keep up with the Joneses, don't we?

BROWN. What kind of men had you in mind?

SIR HORACE. Well, it seems to an outsider that you haven't anything like your proper amount of Fellowships. Particularly on what I might call the side of the future.

JAGO. By which you mean science?

SIR HORACE. By which I mean science. You haven't anything like enough Fellowships for scientists and engineers. And this country is dead unless the universities can find them and train them. I should like to see you have many more young scientific Fellows. They're the chaps you want. (*He picks up his drink*)

JAGO. That's most interesting.

SIR HORACE. You're doubtful, Dr Jago.

JAGO. I'm a little uncertain how much you want to alter us. If you swamped us with science—you see, I'm at a disadvantage. I haven't the faintest idea of the scale of benefaction you feel we need.

SIR HORACE. I was only thinking aloud. But imagine that people of my way of thought were trying to help the college with—a fairly considerable sum . . .

CHRYSTAL (*briskly*) A Fellowship costs fifty thousand.

SIR HORACE. What was that, Mr Chrystal?

CHRYSTAL. It needs a capital endowment of fifty thousand pounds to pay for a Fellowship today.

SIR HORACE. Well, imagine that a few people could see their way to providing a few of those units.

JAGO. If they were giving them for Fellowships in general, it would be perfect, but if the Fellowships were restricted to science . . . (*He breaks off*)

SIR HORACE. Yes?

JAGO. It might raise difficulties.

SIR HORACE. I don't quite see them.

BROWN. I think the Senior Tutor means, Sir Horace, that on the book today we've got four scientific Fellows out of thirteen. Of course, none of us would maintain that was the right proportion.

JAGO. No, but if we changed it drastically at a single stroke, it would alter the place overnight. It would change the character of our society.

SIR HORACE (*with sudden energy*) You will have to change the character of your society. History will make you. Life will make you. You won't be able to stop it, Dr Jago. You know what I mean?

JAGO. Then we lose our identity.

SIR HORACE. Not lose it. Change it. You can't remain an intellectual island for ever.

JAGO (*with a burst of emotion*) No, of course we can't. And nobody wants that. This country needs science, of course it does. But not *merely* science, not *solely* science. What a bleak future that would be. An exclusively technological race. Surely we need knowledge—expert knowledge—*of every kind*. And not just knowledge, but vision and passion, imagination, the things of the spirit, philosophy and creative art. *All* human genius is not scientific. *All* human genius is not even rational. We need men of broad sympathies—men of high culture—men of the widest possible range. *Educated* men in the deepest sense—surely *that's* our need—if the frightening flood of science isn't to put what's left of civilization into the hands of the wrong sort of men—factory men, technological men, commercial men without real education. You see the danger?

SIR HORACE (*with good humour*) I should—I'm one myself.

JAGO. I hope it doesn't need saying that I wasn't talking of men like you, sir.

SIR HORACE (*with a smile*) Weren't you?

JAGO. No. You're an exceptional man.

SIR HORACE. Thank you. But wouldn't it be true to say that any man elected to a Fellowship must also be an exceptional man?

JAGO. By no means. He must have exceptional knowledge in his subject. I suppose in varying degrees you could say that of everyone you have met here tonight, but I doubt if one of us would claim to be an exceptional man.

SIR HORACE. I think I have been listening to one—and with great interest. I shall think over what you have said, Dr Jago. In any case, far be it from me to interfere in the internal affairs of your society. My thought of increasing you scientifically was—well, just a thought.

(NEWBY *enters up* L *and crosses to Sir Horace*)

BROWN (*eagerly*) And an exceedingly generous thought.

CHRYSTAL. Yes, indeed.

BROWN. I'm sure we should all be most profoundly grateful if Sir Horace could . . .

SIR HORACE (*to Newby*) Yes?

NEWBY. Your car is here, sir.

SIR HORACE. Thank you.

(NEWBY *exits up* L)

(*He rises*) Gentlemen, it's been a delightful evening.

(CHRYSTAL, BROWN *and* JAGO *rise*)

I can't tell you how valuable I've found it to have your opinions.
BROWN. Must you go so soon?
SIR HORACE. I'm flying to Hamburg in the morning.
CHRYSTAL. I'm sorry you couldn't stay the night. We should have liked to have made you comfortable.
BROWN (*quickly*) As comfortable as our means allow.
SIR HORACE. I'm sure you would have done me handsomely, but I must get back. I don't want to disturb Mrs Royce. (*He moves up* c)

(CHRYSTAL *crosses to* L *of Sir Horace.* JAGO *and* BROWN *move above the table* RC)

Please say good-bye to her for me. (*He stops and turns*) By the way, I heard a rumour about her husband. I'm glad it's not true.
JAGO (*moving to* R *of Sir Horace*) I'm afraid it is.
SIR HORACE. Oh, dear. (*He pauses briefly*) Who will be your next Master?
BROWN. He's standing next to you, Sir Horace.
SIR HORACE. Dr Jago? That's a fascinating choice. (*He moves up* R *of the table* LC)

(CHRYSTAL *moves up* L *of the table* LC. JAGO *moves up* C)

Good night, gentlemen. We'll be in touch.
CHRYSTAL. I'll see you to the car.
JAGO
BROWN } (*together*) Good night, Sir Horace.

(SIR HORACE *moves up* LC *then stops, turns and looks upwards*)

SIR HORACE. Jago. Right up there among the stars—that's where science is putting man.
JAGO (*gently*) But he's been there ever since time, Sir Horace.

(SIR HORACE *smiles and exits up* L.
CHRYSTAL *follows him off*)

(*He moves down* C. *Ruefully*) Have I dished the benefaction?
BROWN. No. He liked you. Couldn't you tell? You may have pulled off a miracle.

(*The church clock strikes the half-hour.*
NIGHTINGALE *enters from the Lodge*)

In any case, you had every right to express a view—and one with which I largely agree. Indeed, as our next Master, you had more than a right, you had a duty to speak for the college.
NIGHTINGALE. Jago. I think you should know your majority has been broken. I've decided to vote for Crawford. Good night.

(NIGHTINGALE *exits up* L. JAGO *stares after him for a moment then turns to Brown as*—

the CURTAIN *falls*

D

SCENE 2

SCENE—*The same. Ten minutes later.*

When the CURTAIN *rises,* GAY *is apparently asleep in the deck-chair.* WINSLOW *is standing above the table* RC. BROWN *is* R *of Winslow.* LEWIS *is standing above the table* LC. CHRYSTAL *is* R *of the table* LC, *serving punch.* DESPARD-SMITH *is* L *of the table* LC.

CHRYSTAL. Despard, another glass? (*He hands a glass of punch across the table to Despard-Smith then moves* C) Winslow, punch?

WINSLOW. Thank you, I prefer not to mix my refreshment, when taking wine with the enemy.

BROWN. Enemy? Oh, come . . .

WINSLOW. Very well—the opposition.

(LEWIS *moves up* R *of Chrystal*)

CHRYSTAL. That's better. Whatever our differences, we all have the same objective.

WINSLOW. And what, pray, is that?

CHRYSTAL. The good of the college.

GETLIFFE. Quite.

DESPARD-SMITH. H-hear, hear! (*He sneezes*)

WINSLOW (*sitting above the table* RC) An unexceptional sentiment. However, I doubt the dean has brought the two camps together merely to platitudinize.

(BROWN *moves to* R *of the table* RC. LEWIS *moves above Winslow.* GETLIFFE *moves down* R *of the table* LC. DESPARD-SMITH *moves down* L *of the table* LC)

CHRYSTAL (*with a step towards Winslow*) I haven't. Gentlemen, we must face the position about this election.

(DESPARD-SMITH *coughs*)

GAY (*opening his eyes*) Bronchitis. I warned you.

DESPARD-SMITH (*irritably*) Oh, go to sleep.

GAY. Sleep? When you're having a pow-wow about the election? No, I'm wide awake and sharp as mustard. Pray continue.

CHRYSTAL. Gentlemen, there are only two candidates for the Mastership. As things now stand, neither will be elected.

LEWIS   ⎫   ⎧What?
WINSLOW ⎬ (*together*) ⎨I beg your pardon?
GETLIFFE ⎭   ⎩You can't be certain of that.

CHRYSTAL. I can. I am. A simple majority won't do. The trouble is our ancient statute. According to the statute . . .

GAY (*abruptly*) No hanky-panky. (*He struggles to his feet*)

(GETLIFFE *moves to* R *of the table* LC)

No tampering with the statute. I won't have it.

CHRYSTAL. My dear Gay, I was not . . .

GAY. No statute can be changed without a meeting of all Fellows presided over by the Master.

CHRYSTAL (*moving down* C *and facing Gay*) I had no intention . . .

GAY. Yes, you had, you had every intention. The statute lays it down that a Master cannot be elected without a majority of all Fellows. *All* fellows. Yes, indeed. None of your five-four, six-five jiggery-pokery. There are thirteen Fellows in this college. I shall not declare a master elected until I am satisfied he is clearly supported by seven votes.

CHRYSTAL. If you will allow me . . .

GAY. I will not. They tried your trick in sixteen-eighty-four. Started a scare that the plague had broken out at Ely. It emptied the college overnight—except for the two scoundrels who planned it. One elected the other Master. The Master made the other Dean. I'm glad to say both were dumped in the river with a copy of the old statute round their necks. Let that be a warning to you. (*He moves to the Lodge door and turns*) Come along, Despard. Time for bed.

DESPARD-SMITH. I am remaining.

GAY. Asking for pneumonia. Positively demanding it.

(GAY *shuffles off into the Lodge*)

DESPARD-SMITH. He's not all there.

WINSLOW. I trust there's no more of him anywhere else.

(CHRYSTAL *reacts and moves up* C)

BROWN (*sitting* R *of the table* RC) Were you proposing to change the statute, Dean?

CHRYSTAL (*moving down* C) Of course not. I was merely pointing out the position.

WINSLOW. Which is?

CHRYSTAL. Stalemate. Thanks to Nightingale it's six-five. Thanks to the statute it must be seven for one of them. The two candidates can't vote for themselves, so obviously they'll abstain. That being so, I see no chance of another vote for either. Do you?

GETLIFFE } (*together*) { No.
LEWIS   }   { What happens then?

BROWN. In the event of the college failing to elect, the new Master is appointed by the Visitor.

LEWIS (*moving between Brown and Winslow*) Who is the Visitor?

GETLIFFE. Our local bishop.

DESPARD-SMITH (*gloomily*) A l-lamentable incumbent. No sense of humour.

CHRYSTAL. Nonetheless, we may be forced to turn to him—and if that happens, one thing is clear. It won't mean your candidate getting in. He's an unbeliever.

WINSLOW. And it won't mean yours. Academically he's a non-entity.

CHRYSTAL. Without agreeing, you make my point. It will mean a third party foisted on us. The bishop will name someone from outside the college.

GETLIFFE (*moving below the table; to Despard-Smith*) What do you think?

DESPARD-SMITH. I'm bound to say the Dean is right.

CHRYSTAL. Do you want that?

GETLIFFE. I don't.

BROWN. Nor I.

DESPARD-SMITH. I should consider it a c-catastrophe.

CHRYSTAL. Very well. I'm going to make a suggestion which will save us from the Visitor.

WINSLOW. Bring it to a point, my dear Dean.

CHRYSTAL (*bluntly*) We tell the two candidates they must vote for each other.

GETLIFFE. What?

CHRYSTAL. We tell them we will not tolerate this matter going to the Visitor. That voting for each other is the only way of bringing the required majority of seven within reach of either.

LEWIS. And if they refuse?

CHRYSTAL. We'll threaten them with a third candidate. Someone we decide on, not an outsider fobbed off on us by the bishop. *We'll* choose him, from amongst ourselves.

(*There is a pause*)

WINSLOW. I must say it's a beautiful thought.

GETLIFFE (*moving to R of the table LC*) It doesn't look unreasonable.

DESPARD-SMITH. It's absolutely unp-precedented.

(LEWIS *moves down R of Brown*)

WINSLOW. I take it it hasn't escaped you, Dean, that if Pilbrow returns from his travels in time, your candidate commands a probable six votes—and Crawford's will neatly get him home?

CHRYSTAL. True, but it gives your man a chance. It means he'll only need one more vote to win. If someone else crosses over, your man wins. If not, it's ours. Either way, we're saved from the Visitor. Well, gentlemen?

WINSLOW. Ingenious. I'm looking for the catch.

CHRYSTAL. There is no catch. In this we're allies.

WINSLOW. Even the idyllic spectacle of the lion lying down with the lamb does not entirely reconcile me to the Dean's idea. However . . .

CHRYSTAL. Agreed?

WINSLOW. Agreed.

GETLIFFE. Good man.

LEWIS. Who's going to tell the candidates?

GETLIFFE. This calls for tact.

WINSLOW. In that case, forgive me, I shan't volunteer.

GETLIFFE
CHRYSTAL } (*turning to Brown; together*) Arthur.
LEWIS

BROWN. Yes, all right. I'll do it.

(BROWN *rises, crosses and exits to the Lodge.* GETLIFFE *moves to* L *of the table* LC *and helps himself to punch*)

DESPARD-SMITH. Supposing they t-turn us down, who is our third candidate to be?

CHRYSTAL (*sitting* L *of the table* RC) Let's go down the fellows in order of seniority.

(LEWIS *sits* R *of the table* RC)

Gay—Pilbrow. Over age. You, Despard. The statutes won't let us have you, either, I'm afraid.

DESPARD-SMITH. Some men of s-seventy are still competent to hold high office . . .

CHRYSTAL. You would be. No-one doubts it. But it can't happen.

DESPARD-SMITH. I've had a disappointing life. It's a s-scandalous story. I ought to have been asked to take on the b-burden fourteen years ago. I tell you, the college would have been a d-different place.

CHRYSTAL. Yes, quite. Going on down the list . . .

DESPARD-SMITH. People here have never shown me the s-slightest consideration. (*He moves to* R *of the table* LC) Any punch left?

GETLIFFE. Yes, I think so. (*He fills a glass for Despard-Smith*)

DESPARD-SMITH. One big disappointment, that's my life. I regard my future as c-c-disastrous.

(GETLIFFE *hands the drink to* DESPARD-SMITH *who lapses into a sulky silence*)

CHRYSTAL (*grimly*) Going on down the list. Winslow, you're the next.

WINSLOW. Curiously enough, I was aware of that.

CHRYSTAL. Do you think your health would be up to the job?

WINSLOW. Your concern for my welfare is most affecting.

GETLIFFE (*moving below the table* LC) I seriously doubt whether it would be fair to ask you.

WINSLOW. What you mean is, I'm temperamentally unsuited.

GETLIFFE. Not at all, my dear fellow. Just the same . . .

WINSLOW. And you're perfectly right. I am scarcely a success with my colleagues as Bursar. As Master I should be, like the deputy's future, disastrous.

(BROWN *enters from the Lodge*)

BROWN. Well, I've told them.

CHRYSTAL. And?

BROWN (*crossing to* R *of Getliffe*) I don't know. There's an argument. Jago is saying . . .

(LUKE *strides in up* L *at top speed. He wears his oldest clothes and has obviously come straight from the laboratory*)

LUKE (*crossing to* R *of Brown*) My God, I've stood just about as much as I can stand of this man Nightingale.

CHRYSTAL. What's happened.

LUKE. I just got back from the Cavendish. I passed Nightingale at the gate. I gather he's switched to Crawford.

CHRYSTAL. Yes.

LUKE. Well, that's his business, though I've got my thoughts on that sort of thing. He as good as told me that unless I switched, too, he'd see that my Fellowship's not made a permanency.

BROWN. I shouldn't pay too much attention.

LUKE (*facing Brown*) Do you think I did? I told him I'd see him in hell first, and the bloody man said a docker's son shouldn't be here, anyway, and I'd be more at home in a Polytechnic.

LEWIS }
BROWN } (*together*) { Good God!
{ He said *what?*

LUKE (*moving to* L *of Winslow*) I should like to be kept in this college, it's much nicer than the old dockyard, but if you and your bunch think that I can be blackmailed because I'm afraid to lose my comforts, you can think again. (*He moves up* C) I just wanted you to know.

LEWIS (*to Getliffe; indignantly*) Look, Francis, you can't let Nightingale get away with this.

GETLIFFE (*at once*) No, I'll stop it. (*He moves to* L *of Luke*) I'm sorry, Walter. It shouldn't have happened. I needn't tell you that nothing of this kind will affect your future.

DESPARD-SMITH (*moving to* L *of Getliffe*) I associate myself with you, Getliffe.

(CRAWFORD *and* JAGO *enter from the Lodge.* CRAWFORD *is relaxed and smoking a cigar.* JAGO *is white and tense*)

CRAWFORD (*moving below the deck-chair*) Well, gentlemen.

(JAGO *stands down* L *of Crawford*)

The senior tutor and I have had a word together about your little *demarche.*

DESPARD-SMITH (*moving and standing between Winslow and Chrystal*) And w-what is your answer?

JAGO. We accept your ultimatum.

BROWN. Ultimatum? Oh, come . . .

CHRYSTAL. I'm very glad to hear it, Jago.

CRAWFORD. If there are no other candidates, we shall vote for each other. Speaking as a private person, I think I take a mild exception to the way you've forced our hand over this. Jago and

I had just agreed to abstain from voting. However, that's past history. The matter's settled.

Jago (*tensely*) For my part, I have something more to say.

Crawford. I should leave it. You'll only take it out of yourself.

Jago (*crossing down L of Chrystal*) I'm sorry, but I take the strongest exception to the way this has been done. Apparently you consider that one of us is fit to be your Master. I should have hoped that in the meantime you might treat us as responsible persons.

Brown. We were anxious to get everything in order. None of us knows how much time we've got left.

Jago. That's no reason for treating Crawford and me like college servants.

Winslow. Since when have college servants been required to vote for each other?

Jago (*controlling himself with difficulty*) Anyone who stands for office is fair game for any kind of jibe. You've taught me that lesson. (*He crosses to L of the table LC*) I shall vote for Crawford.

Getliffe. Good work.

(Despard-Smith *crosses to R of the table LC*)

Crawford (*moving L*) There's nothing further to say.

Winslow (*rising and crossing above Chrystal to L of him*) In that case, if the Dean has no more permutations to offer, I'll seek out our hostess and say my farewells.

Chrystal (*rising*) Good night, Winslow.

Winslow. I still think there's a catch.

Chrystal. No, no, I assure you.

Brown. Good night, Godfrey.

Crawford. Coming, Jago?

Jago. I want a word with Chrystal and Brown.

Winslow (*crossing to R of Crawford*) It might generate a shade less heat if we invited you both to submit a prospectus.

(Crawford *and* Winslow *move towards the Lodge door*)

Crawford. You're electing a Master, you know, not an hotel manager.

Winslow. If the college is misguided enough to elect Dr Jago, I shall beg to be excused if I fail to remember the distinction.

(Winslow *and* Crawford *exit to the Lodge.* Luke *moves up* L *to go*)

Getliffe (*following Luke*) Look here, if Nightingale ever threatens you again, I want you to come straight to me and tell me.

Luke. Can I wring his neck first and tell you afterwards?

(Getliffe *and* Luke *exit up* L)

Despard-Smith (*moving down LC; to Lewis*) Whoever wins, I foresee disaster.

LEWIS (*rising and crossing to* C) That's interesting.
DESPARD-SMITH. The college has only itself to blame. They should have made me M-Master years ago.

(LEWIS *and* DESPARD-SMITH *exit to the Lodge.* JAGO *crosses and stands up* L *of the table* RC. CHRYSTAL *moves* C)

JAGO. I should have been told about this. I should have been told at the first mention of this piece of—persuasion.
CHRYSTAL. I don't see why.
JAGO. When I find my party negotiating behind my back . . .
CHRYSTAL. This isn't a party matter, it's a college matter.
JAGO. I'm sorry. I'm not used to having my actions dictated. Before my friends arrange to do so, I expect them to tell me first.
BROWN (*crossing to* R *of Jago*) I think you're forgetting, Paul, that something very notable has been achieved. You're standing with a clear majority again. It's seven-six in your favour—and you owe it entirely to the Dean.

(*There is a pause*)

JAGO. I'm sorry. Your heads are cooler than mine. This thing's like mountain-climbing—when you're in sight of the summit and you know that one false step—it frays the nerves. It's an astonishing manœuvre. I'm more grateful, Dean, than I can say.
CHRYSTAL. I'm glad it came off.
BROWN. We'll make you master, yet. And now, my dear Paul, let's sleep on it.
JAGO. I shan't sleep tonight. You go along.
BROWN (*concerned*) Try to relax. It's going to be all right, you know.
JAGO. If Pilbrow comes.

(CHRYSTAL *moves up* L)

BROWN. He'll come. He'll come.

(JAGO *forces a smile*)

(*He moves to Chrystal*) He's not a simple character.
CHRYSTAL. I give you that. By God, I give you that.

(CHRYSTAL *and* BROWN *exit up* L. *There is a pause.* JAGO *wanders up* C *and looks up at the topmost branches of the tree.*
VERNON ROYCE, *the Master, enters from the Lodge, and moves below the deck-chair. He is in his sixties, no more. His eyes are sunken and his flesh dried, but his voice is still reasonably strong. He wears pyjamas, slippers and dressing-gown*)

MASTER (*watching Jago*) Up, up, up—to the top of the tree.
JAGO (*turning; startled*) Master! (*He moves down* R *of the table* LC)
MASTER. Not so loud. I'm playing hookey. (*He crosses carefully to* RC) On the whole, you know, women are gentle creatures, and even

occasionally open to reason, but let them get you on a sick-bed and the mildest of them become Martinets. (*He lowers himself into the chair above the table* RC) I've just sent Muriel down to the Backs to look for my daughter.

Jago. She went off with Roy Calvert.

Master. I know she did. They're under the willows. I spotted them from my bedroom window so I've sent my dear wife in the opposite direction. If they play possum they're safe for a spell—and so am I. Is that brandy punch?

Jago. Yes.

Master. Pour me a glass, there's a good chap.

Jago (*moving* c) Do you think you should?

Master. My dear man, what difference can it conceivably make?

(Jago *stares at the Master*)

Well, of course I know. I've known for weeks. But I must ask you not to let Muriel know that I know. Not only would it distress her dreadfully, but I'd feel as if I'd been caught cheating at cards. You see, we're playing a game, my wife and I—it's called, "The Master mustn't know he's dying"—and as it's the last game I'll ever play, I'd really rather like to win.

Jago. Dying? What on earth gave you that idea?

Master. Look, Jago, it's a little tiring, this pretending. I don't mind doing it for my family but I don't have to pretend to you, so if you don't pretend to me, either, we might have a decent conversation.

(*The church clock strikes the hour.* Jago *goes to the table* LC, *fills a glass with punch and gives it to the Master*)

(*He takes a drink*) Stronger this year—or is it just that I'm weaker?

Jago. No, it's stronger. (*He moves* c) I'll get a rug.

Master. Why? Are you cold? Stop fussing, man, or I'll go back to bed, and I came down specially to see you. Come and sit here, beside me.

(Jago *sits* L *of the table* RC)

I gather from the grape-vine—a word here and a whisper there—none of which I'm supposed to have heard, by the by—I gather you're to be my successor. Well, is that so? Or have I been listening at keyholes for nothing?

Jago. I'm in the running.

Master. Will you get it?

Jago. I don't know. The college is deeply—passionately—divided.

Master. The in-fighting as bitter as ever, eh? I wonder why people imagine that academics are less passionate than other people. It's quite untrue.

JAGO. I think it's because most scholarship is conducted with much private devotion and unseen passion. When the clash comes, all this submerged emotion comes bursting out, and people are astonished.

MASTER. I remember my election. The blood-letting was venomous. I rather enjoyed it.

JAGO. But *you* didn't care whether you won or lost.

MASTER. Not particularly. Do you?

JAGO (*intensely*) Yes.

MASTER. You want to be Master?

JAGO. I think I want it more than anything in the world. It's strange. When I was a young man I wanted everything a man could want. Honour, riches, the love of women. Such dreams—such fine, proud dreams one has, when one's young. But the years go by and the vision narrows. You no longer see yourself as Shakespeare—Leonardo—the next Prime Minister. The range of ambition dwindles down. But the thrust and drive is as fierce as ever. A man mayn't cry any more for the moon, but what he *still* desires, the *final* longing, *that* he wants more desperately than ever. This is what I have come to want. The Mastership of this lovely place. To lose myself in its service. To devote my last energies to making it a perfect thing. That's why I want it. At least, that's why I tell myself I want it. Sometimes I think all I want is to hear them call me Master.

MASTER. It doesn't matter, you know. It's quite unimportant.

JAGO. I know. I'm disgusted with myself for getting so excited about something that doesn't matter in the least.

MASTER. Crawford's your rival, isn't he?

JAGO. Yes.

MASTER. Scientists are too bumptious. Who's running your party?

JAGO. Chrystal and Brown.

MASTER. Chrystal the king-maker. You know, it's remarkable. People always believe that, if only they support the successful candidate, they've got his backing for ever. It's an illusion. I assure you one feels a certain faint irritation at the faces of one's loyal supporters. They catch one's eye and smirk. But perhaps you've discovered that already.

JAGO. Gratitude plays queer tricks at times.

MASTER. Gratitude isn't an emotion. But the expectation of gratitude is a very lively one. Tell me—(*he leans forward eagerly*) I don't have many pleasures left, but one of them is watching the human comedy—tell me, when do they think I'm going to bow out? Well, come on, man, out with it. You understand, I'm fascinated.

JAGO (*after a pause*) They expect to get the election over before the next academic year.

MASTER. I must do my best not to upset their calculations. (*He hands his glass to Jago*) Give me another glass, would you?

JAGO. Are you in pain?

Master. No, no. A little discomfort, that's all. One shrivels up like an autumn leaf.

Jago. Don't!

Master. It seems quite natural, I assure you—and it's surprisingly easy to face.

Jago (*rising*) Not for me. I find it intolerable. (*He moves to the table* LC *and refills the Master's glass*)

Master. Do you?

(Jago *hands the Master his drink*)

Thank you, Jago. (*He drinks*) You and I never really got on, did we? But now, at the limit of life, we're friends.

Jago. Master, don't you think you should go in?

Master. In a moment. It's pleasant, sitting here. You know, however impervious one is to the past, there are times when one is drugged by it. The stones in the courtyards, the panelling in Hall, the view over the roofs to King's. All these have been so long the same. We go. They remain. Strangely enough, it's a comforting thought. (*He pauses*) Jago.

Jago. Yes.

Master. I have no vote—not even a posthumous one—but I hope you get it.

Jago. There are times when I feel quite certain I shall get it— and others when I think it will be taken from me at the last.

Master. They say if you want something enough, it's yours.

Jago. But if you want it too much? (*He pauses*) I really think you should go in, now, Master. (*He moves to the Master*) It's turned quite chilly.

Master. You're worse than Muriel.

Jago. Take my arm.

(*The* Master *rises on Jago's arm*)

Master. One thing. If you don't get it, don't brood. It's better to light candles than curse the darkness.

(Jago *leads the* Master *towards the Lodge door*)

That's not original. Will you remember?

(Jago *stops*)

Jago. What are you trying to tell me?

Master. Nothing. You're going up—up, up—to the top of the tree.

Jago *and the* Master *go together into the Lodge as—*

the Curtain *falls*

ACT III

Scene i

SCENE—*The Combination Room. A month later. Late afternoon.*

When the CURTAIN *rises, it is a dull day and a storm is brewing. The window up* LC *is open. The curtains are not yet drawn, nor the lights on. The table up* C *is laid with silver tea-things and cups, plates, cake, etc., for tea. There is some slight alteration to the furniture. The table down* L *has been removed. The chess-table is in the corner up* L *and an upright chair* R *of it. The other upright chair from down* R *is now* L *of the table up* R. *The tub chair* RC *is in the corner down* R. GAY, LEWIS, CALVERT *and* WINSLOW *are finishing tea.* WINSLOW *is seated at the right end of the table.* LEWIS *is seated below the right end of the table.* CALVERT *is standing above the table, pouring a cup of tea.* GAY *is seated* L *of the table. He has a white napkin tucked into his collar and is nearing the end of a hearty meal.*

GAY. How are you getting on, Eliot? Have you had one of these lemon-curd tarts?

LEWIS. I have.

GAY. I congratulate you. Calvert, have a slice of this excellent stick-jaw cake.

CALVERT (*sitting on the centre chair above the table*) Too heavy for me, sir.

GAY. Ah, that was a fine tea. That was a tea and a half. I have never believed in fasting after a funeral. Merely because one fills one's stomach does not mean one grieves the less. Five Masters I've buried since I became a Fellow—and five excellent teas I've eaten afterwards. But I grieve for poor Royce, indeed I do. He was stricken with the disease, which, as my old saga men would say, was his bane. He bore it as valiantly as they would have borne it and he had indeed one consolation not granted to many of them. He died in the certainty of our Christian faith. But we cannot always look back. Forward! That's the place to look. (*He removes his napkin, rises and moves down* LC) I must write my notice of the vacancy.

WINSLOW (*rising and moving to* R *of Gay*) Quite unnecessary. (*He takes a sheet of paper from his pocket*) I've got one here. I had it typed in the bursary this morning.

GAY. Typed? I'm not sure it oughtn't to be in my own hand. I can't get out of the responsibility for any slips, you know.

WINSLOW. There are no slips. (*He hands the notice to Gay*)

GAY. Let me read it.

(Winslow *sits in the armchair down* c)

(*He reads*) "Owing to the death of Mr Vernon Royce there is a vacancy in the office of Master of this College." No argument about that. "The fellows will meet in convocation to elect a new Master, according to Statutes B to F, at ten o'clock in the morning of July the second." The second? You haven't made a slip there, I suppose?

Winslow (*impatiently*) The vacancy occurred in term. It is fourteen days from today.

Gay (*moving and sitting at the desk* l) Well, that seems fair enough. Now, all it needs is my signature.

Winslow. It doesn't.

Gay. Well, it's going to get it. (*He takes out an ancient fountain pen and laboriously signs the notice*)

Calvert (*to Lewis*) I saw Jago at the gate. He looked ravaged.

Winslow. With grief or hope?

Lewis. Now, Godfrey . . .

Gay (*as he signs*) ". . . Gay. Senior fellow." There. (*He rises and moves to the notice-board*) That's a fine notice. Now I must fix it.

Calvert. Let me do it for you.

Gay (*pinning the notice on the board*) Not a bit of it, my dear chap, not a bit of it. There's life in the old dog yet. Ah, that's well done. Anyone can see with half an eye there's a vacancy.

(Gay *exits* l)

Calvert. Any sign of Pilbrow, yet?

Lewis. Not yet.

Calvert. A fortnight left. He's running it fine.

Lewis. He'll come.

(Jago *enters* r *and moves* rc)

(*He rises and moves to* l *of Jago*) I looked for you after the service.

Jago. I wanted to collect my thoughts. I went for a walk.

Lewis. Where?

Jago. Over Coe fen to Grantchester and on by the back of the river. There was no-one about. Just a single swan moving on the water. (*He pauses*) It's hard to accept he's dead.

Calvert. Yes.

(Brown *enters* l, *carrying a sheaf of papers.* Jago *and* Lewis *turn to him*)

Brown (*moving* lc) I've just got the examination results. I hope we haven't had too many disasters. (*He searches for a name in the papers*) Thank God!

Jago (*crossing to* r *of Brown*) What's happened?

Brown. Young Timberlake's through. They've given him a Third.

(Calvert *rises*)

Which, between you and me, is probably more than abstract justice required. Still, I think Sir Horace will be satisfied. If the young man had crashed it could have been the most expensive failure in the history of the college.

JAGO. May I see them?

(BROWN *hands the paper to* JAGO *who sits on the chair below the right end of the table and spreads the papers out on the table in front of him.* BROWN *sits* L *of Jago, below the table.* CALVERT *moves to* R *of Jago.* LEWIS *moves behind Jago. He and* CALVERT *look over Jago's shoulder.* WINSLOW *sits motionless.*

DESPARD-SMITH *enters* L, *clutching a similar sheaf of papers*)

DESPARD-SMITH (*moving to* L *of the table up* C) The results are out. Ah, I see you've g-got them. Taking the rough with the s-smooth, I think we can be reasonably satisfied with the achievements of the men. What do you say, Senior Tutor?

JAGO (*studying the results*) I go further. We can be proud of them.

WINSLOW (*quietly*) I wonder, Senior Tutor, if you would be so kind as to look for my son's name. Winslow, R. You'll find it under the W's at the end of the list. No, I must amplify. Knowing my son, you'll find it at the very end of the end of the list.

(JAGO *searches the papers.* DESPARD-SMITH *moves up* L)

JAGO (*at length; looking up*) I don't seem to be able . . . (*He rises and moves* C) I'll ring up the examiners straight away. I did once find a name left out by mistake. (*He catches Despard-Smith's eye*)

(DESPARD-SMITH *shakes his head*)

WINSLOW. Thank you. That won't be necessary. (*He bows his head*)

(*All but* JAGO *turn away, embarrassed.* DESPARD-SMITH *moves to the notice-board.* CALVERT *and* LEWIS *move to the window up* C *and stand gazing out*)

JAGO (*moving swiftly to* R *of Winslow*) I'm very sorry, Winslow.

WINSLOW. Pray don't distress yourself on my account.

JAGO. And I'm dreadfully sorry you had to hear it in public. When one's unhappy, it's intolerable to be watched.

WINSLOW (*with a glance at the others*) They're feeling I've been taken down a peg. They're saying how arrogant and rude I've been.

JAGO (*sitting on the left arm of the armchair* RC) "They" don't matter. None of us matters.

WINSLOW. There's something in what they're saying—as you should know more than most. If I were capable of an apology, I would make one. You'll have to take the will for the deed.

JAGO. My dear Winslow . . .

WINSLOW (*simply*) He's rather a nice boy—my son. A fool—but nice. He's just got engaged.

Jago. That's splendid news.
Winslow (*with a sudden return to his old manner*) We scarcely know the girl. I hope it's all right.

(Chrystal *strides in* l)

Chrystal (*moving down* lc; *briskly*) Well, gentlemen, this is a day.
Brown. Young Timberlake's through.
Chrystal. Yes, and someone must have tipped Sir Horace the wink. I've just got this. (*He takes a letter from his pocket*)

(Lewis *moves down* r. Calvert *moves down* r *of the table up* c)

(*He reads*) "My dear Dean, during the past year you and I have had one or two talks about the future of the college. I've also had the privilege of hearing the views of Dr Jago and Mr Brown. Feeling as I do its invaluable benefits to my nephew and the great part I can see it playing in the world, I am clear that the most useful assistance anyone can give the College is the endowment of Fellowships. Accordingly I should be honoured to transfer to you a capital sum of three hundred thousand pounds——"

(Calvert *whistles and moves* c. Brown *rises*)

"——which I take to be the equivalent of six Fellowships. Five of these Fellowships are to be devoted to scientific and engineering subjects and one is to be held in any subject the College thinks fit. I shall crystallize my ideas further if I learn that the general scheme is acceptable to the College, and in particular to your new Master, on whose co-operation in carrying it out we shall all depend. Yours very sincerely, Horace Timberlake." Well, Arthur, we've done something between us.
Brown (*moving to* r *of Chrystal*) This is the largest benefaction in the history of the college.

(Jago *rises, moves behind the downstage chair* c *of the table and faces up* c)

Jago. It's going to make a difference to us. It's going to change us.
Chrystal (*firmly*) I call this a day.
Despard-Smith (*moving to* l *of Chrystal*) It will need the most serious consideration before the college could possibly decide to accept.
Calvert (*leaning on the back of the armchair* rc) Somehow I rather think we shall.
Lewis. Of course we shall. Congratulations, Dean.
Chrystal (*crossing and sitting on the edge of the desk* l) Brown's more responsible than I. Without Brown we shouldn't have come within shouting distance.
Brown. I disagree. When I think of the boundless time and trouble the Dean has bestowed upon securing this benefaction, I

believe we ought to rank the Dean himself among the great benefactors of this society.

DESPARD-SMITH (*bleakly*) I associate myself with you, Brown. (*He
moves and sits on the chair* L *of the table up* C)

CALVERT. The old boy has certainly unbelted to some purpose.
I wonder how many free dinners he could have taken off us before
we gave up?

WINSLOW (*quite still*) Correct me if I am wrong—I gather some
members of the College have been discussing a benefaction with Sir
Horace Timberlake?

(CHRYSTAL *rises.* JAGO *looks away*)

BROWN (*quickly*) In the vaguest terms you can possibly imagine.
Sir Horace asked one or two questions and it wouldn't have been
ordinary decent manners not to reply. (*He moves up* R *to Chrystal*) I
imagine the Dean was placed in the same embarrassing position.

WINSLOW. It must have been extremely embarrassing. I take it,
my dear Tutor, you and the Dean were reluctantly forced to discuss
the finances of the College?

(CALVERT *circles up* RC *to* L *of Lewis*)

BROWN. Naturally we shouldn't consider ourselves competent.
(*He moves to the armchair* LC *and sits*) I recall very vividly one evening
when the Dean asked me what I thought was the point of Sir Horace's
questions: "I suppose it can't mean money," he said. "If I had the
slightest hope it might"—I think I'm remembering him correctly—
"our first step would be to bring the Bursar in."

WINSLOW. I'm very much affected by that reminiscence. I'm also
very much affected by the thought of the Dean expending "boundless time and trouble" without dreaming for a moment that there
would be any question of money.

CHRYSTAL (*moving* LC) My dear Winslow . . .

BROWN. I'm sure I'm speaking for the Dean as well as myself
when I say that nothing would distress us more than that the Bursar
should feel in the slightest degree left out.

CHRYSTAL. It's only the peculiar circumstances . . .

WINSLOW. I've never had much opinion of myself as Bursar.
It's interesting to find others taking the same view. It looks at any
rate as though my judgement remains unimpaired. Which will be
a slight consolation to me in my retirement. (*He rises and moves behind
the armchair* C)

DESPARD-SMITH (*rising*) I hope you're not suggesting . . .

(CHRYSTAL *moves to* L *of Despard-Smith*)

WINSLOW. I'm not suggesting—I'm resigning.

(LEWIS *and* CALVERT *step in to* RC)

BROWN. What?

Winslow. I'm obviously useless when the College goes in for money seriously. It's time the College had someone who can cope with these problems. I resign the Bursarship.

Despard-Smith. This is disastrous.

Chrystal. Come, Winslow, you don't mean this.

Winslow. I resign.

Despard-Smith. No resignation can be accepted while the College is without a M-Master.

Winslow. In that case, the new Master will have a pleasant duty for his first.

Jago (*moving to* L *of the armchair* RC; *suddenly*) This is a wretched exchange.

Chrystal (*sharply*) I don't understand.

Jago. We're exchanging a fine bursar for a rich man's charity.

Chrystal (*moving down* LC) It's not our fault.

Jago. That doesn't make it any more palatable. Winslow, I want you to know that if the choice had lain with me, Sir Horace would have had to find another use for his money. (*He moves to* R *of Winslow*) In one office or another you've guided this College all your life, and in your ten years as Bursar the College has never been so rich.

Winslow. That's no thanks to me. I used to think I wasn't a fool. Sometimes, by the side of my colleagues, I thought I was a remarkably intelligent man. But everything I've touched has come to nothing. (*He crosses to the door* L)

Jago (*following Winslow*) Won't you reconsider?

(Winslow *exits* L.
   Jago *follows him off*)

Calvert (*moving* C) Godfrey will never recover from this.

Despard-Smith. Another disaster for the college.

(Despard-Smith *exits* L)

Brown. If only he'd slept on it.

Chrystal (*moving to* L *of Calvert*) Jago didn't help. What on earth does he mean? "Guided the College all your life." Winslow couldn't guide a two-year-old across the street.

Lewis (*moving* RC) He may have wanted to make a gesture to Winslow.

Calvert. He's bound to be thinking of the election.

Chrystal. He is—too much. And so's his wife. If she doesn't stop playing queen of the castle before they've even lowered the drawbridge, we're sunk. We're probably sunk in any case.

Brown (*sharply*) I don't follow.

Chrystal. Has Pilbrow answered your cables yet?

Brown. Not yet.

Chrystal. I shall expect him when I see him. Sometime next year.

Brown. What do you mean?

E

CHRYSTAL. I mean, you've had no reply from Pilbrow. Without Pilbrow it's six-all and that, my dear Tutor, is not a majority. (*He moves to the door* L)
BROWN (*rising and crossing to Chrystal; thoughtfully*) Dean——

(CHRYSTAL *stops and turns*)

—you're not by any chance letting Sir Horace's cheque affect your attitude to Jago?
CHRYSTAL. Why should it affect it?
BROWN. I just wondered. It hasn't, has it?

(CHRYSTAL *and* BROWN *exit* L)

CALVERT (*moving* LC) I'm wondering, too.
LEWIS. Yes. Roy, I'm suddenly afraid for Jago.
CALVERT. Just so. That gets us nowhere. What's our move?
LEWIS (*moving to Calvert*) Tackle the enemy one by one.
CALVERT. Right.
LEWIS. You know, if he doesn't get it, it won't just be disappointing. It will break his heart.
CALVERT. He's got hold of your imagination.
LEWIS. And yours.

(*The church clock strikes six*)

CALVERT. Yes, blast him. Come on, we'll do our damnedest.

(CALVERT *and* LEWIS *exit* L. *The stage is empty for a moment.*
BIDWELL *and* STRAKER, *college servants, enter* R, *carrying trays.* BIDWELL *moves to* R *of the table up* C *and stacks crockery, etc., on to the tray.* STRAKER *crosses to the window* LC *and looks out*)

STRAKER. Storm coming up. (*He crosses to the switches* L, *switches on the lights, then goes to* L *of the table and stacks crockery, etc., on to his tray*)

(PILBROW *enters* L. *He wears a light travelling coat and carries a hold-all. For all his age, he looks hale and vigorous. He puts the hold-all on the floor up* L)

PILBROW (*removing his coat*) I suppose that tea's stone cold, Straker?
STRAKER. Yes, sir.
BIDWELL. Mr Pilbrow, sir. I'll make some fresh, sir.
PILBROW. Never mind, Bidwell. I'll have a whisky in a minute. Just leave those buns, will you?

(PILBROW *picks up his hold-all, takes it with his coat into the passage off* L *then re-enters*)

BIDWELL. Did you have a good trip, sir?

(STRAKER *exits* R *with his loaded tray*)

Pilbrow. Splendid, thanks. Invigorating. (*He moves to the table up* c *and takes a bun*)

(Bidwell *moves up* r *of the table*)

Well, man, what's the gossip?
Bidwell. You heard about the Master, sir?
Pilbrow. That's why I'm here.
Bidwell. It was a lovely funeral, sir. Very lovely.
Pilbrow. Yes, I'm sorry I missed it. I came at once, but the morning ferry was two hours late.

(Jago *enters* l.
    Bidwell *exits* r *with his loaded tray*)

Jago. Eustace!
Pilbrow (*affectionately*) Paul, my boy.
Jago (*overjoyed*) I heard your voice. I couldn't believe it. Brown's been cabling you all over Europe.

(Bidwell *enters* r *with a crumb-tray and brush and sweeps the table*)

Pilbrow (*munching his bun*) I've been on the move from day to day. Guess where I had lunch yesterday? Split. Split! Ridiculous name. Astonishing number of beautiful girls in Split. (*He sits on the left arm of the armchair* rc) You sit in the market-place and watch them. Why do people get lovelier as you go south from the Brenner? The Tyrolese are lovely. The Dalmatians better still. But they get more prudish as they get more beautiful. I suppose it's a law of nature. A very stupid one.

(Bidwell *laughs, picks up the plate of buns and exits* r)

Well, how are things? You look done up.
Jago. It's been a strain—the Master—and now the election. But I'm better already for seeing you. (*He moves to the armchair* lc *and sits*) We've been counting on getting you back to vote. Chrystal thought you might forget all about it, but I knew you wouldn't let me down.
Pilbrow (*rising*) Paul . . .
Jago. You know, you'll be surprised how well my wife will turn out in the Lodge.

(Bidwell *enters* r *carrying a tray with a bottle of whisky, a syphon of soda and a glass which he puts on the right end of the table up* c)

She always rises to the occasion. She's looking forward to it so very much.
Bidwell. Mr Pilbrow, sir.
Pilbrow. Thank you, Bidwell.
Bidwell. Thank you, sir.

(Bidwell *exits* r)

PILBROW (*moving to Jago*) Paul, I can't do it. I can't vote for you.
JAGO (*stunned*) What's that?
PILBROW. I'm most terribly sorry. I know I've wobbled disgracefully, but Brown rushed me. I've always been fond of you—no excuse, none at all, but—well, I didn't have time to think. Forgive me. (*He moves to the table up* C)

(*There is a pause*)

JAGO (*rising*) What have I done?
PILBROW. Done? Good Lord, man, nothing. It's just that politically we're poles apart and always have been. I can't bear to have anyone say I helped the wrong side. That's all there is to it. (*He pours a drink for himself*)
JAGO (*crossing down* R *of Pilbrow*) What will you do?
PILBROW. Vote for Crawford. Oh, I don't particularly care for him—and you're warm—you've got a great gift of warmth—but politically he's on the right side. That's what matters.
JAGO. Don't human beings matter?
PILBROW. Yes, of course they do.
JAGO. You've always set a value on human beings. Now you're saying you'll just vote for a programme.
PILBROW (*moving to* L *of the armchair* RC) One must sacrifice something . . .
JAGO. If the books you've devoted your life to disappeared to-morrow, Crawford wouldn't notice the difference.
PILBROW. That's probably true, but he stands for the future, whereas . . .
JAGO. You know what this means? You know what you're doing? You're putting him in. You're giving him his majority.
PILBROW. And what if I am? The whole thing's unimportant. Six months from today you'll wonder why you ever gave a damn.
JAGO (*moving* R) You don't understand. Why should you? You've never given a damn whether people elected you to Masterships or Presidencies of Buffaloes' Clubs. You're secure in your scholarship, in your reputation. You're known and admired as a man of letters all over Europe. (*He moves to* R *of Pilbrow*) It's not people like you who are ambitious for office, who need support from outside—it's people like me. I need this job. I need it *intolerably*. For God's sake, let me have it.
PILBROW (*moving and putting his glass on the table up* C; *cheerfully*) What you need is a stiff whisky and a good night's rest. (*He moves to* L *of Jago*) My dear man, a Mastership? Does it matter two hoots? Of *course* it doesn't.

(PILBROW *exits* L. JAGO *is alone for a moment.*
ALICE *enters* R *outside the windows and crosses to the open window* LC)

ALICE (*through the window; breathlessly*) Paul! Oh, thank God I've found you.

Jago (*crossing to the window*) Alice! What is it?

Alice. I asked at the gate—they said your rooms—you weren't there—I had to see you. I . . .

Jago. Come in—come along in. There's nobody here.

(Alice *exits* l *outside the windows.* Jago *closes the window then goes to the door* l *and opens it.*

Alice *enters* l, *crosses to the armchair* lc *and leans on it*)

(*He closes the door, crosses to Alice and tries to calm her*) My dear, my dear, what *is* the matter?

Alice. I don't know how to tell you—Paul, they're saying . . . I can't seem to get my breath . . .

Jago (*leading Alice below the armchair* lc) Come and sit down. Undo your coat.

Alice (*sitting in the armchair* lc) I shouldn't be here.

Jago (r *of her*) Never mind that.

Alice. I'll be all right in a moment—I ran all the way, I . . . Paul, they're saying I'm not fit to go into the Lodge.

Jago. My dear, we've been through all this before. You're imagining things.

Alice. Am I? Did I imagine this? Did I? (*She fumbles in her handbag and pulls out a paper*) There's a whole lot about Crawford—what a fine Master he'd make—and then right at the end . . . Listen. Paul, listen to this. (*She reads*) "Mrs Crawford appears to many members of the college to be well-fitted for the position of Master's wife. *This does not necessarily apply to both candidates' wives.*" That's underlined.

Jago (*taking the paper from her*) Alice, where did you get this?

Alice. It came through the post. It's headed "To all Fellows", but your copy was addressed to me. Paul, I was *meant* to read it.

Jago. It's not signed.

Alice. It was. I crumpled it and the signature came off.

Jago. Whose was it?

Alice. Nightingale's.

Jago (*moving down* rc) Nightingale! What in God's name is he trying to do?

Alice. Get at you through me. Don't you understand? Through me. It's their one chance. I'm your only weakness.

Jago (*moving to her*) My dear . . .

Alice. Of course I am. I'm not a fool. They know you're bound to be elected unless they shout the place down. They think if I know what they're saying about me I won't be able to face it. I'll persuade you to withdraw. (*She rises*) Paul, I felt sick—I didn't know what to do—I ran out of the house . . .

Jago (*putting his arms around her*) Yes, yes, it's all right now.

Alice. I was frightened—I felt hate all round me.

Jago. How could you possibly feel that when I'm here?

Alice. Don't pity me—don't pretend to me.

Jago. I never have.

ALICE. I know I'm an awful woman—clumsy and tactless, but I've never done you as much harm as this. I never thought they'd use me to prevent you being Master.

JAGO. It won't be necessary.

ALICE (*moving below Jago to R of him*) I've been so stupid about the Lodge—looking forward to it—boasting about it—planning parties—(*she moves up RC*) buying that furniture—what shall I do if it's taken away now? (*She sits on the centre chair below the table*) How can I stand what they'll say about me?

JAGO (*moving to L of her*) Alice, I want you to listen to me . . .

ALICE (*hysterically*) Paul, I've never loved anyone but you and all I've done is ruin your career.

JAGO. That's total nonsense. You'll see what nonsense it is if you'll listen. My dear, it seems that I shall be rejected by the college but—wait—not because of anything we've been talking about. Old Eustace Pilbrow has crossed over—for political reasons. He can't possibly have read this—he's been abroad, and anyway he'd be the last to take notice. So, you see, it's not your fault. It's nothing to do with you. Now, will you stop hurting yourself?

ALICE. Oh, thank God! Oh, if it's not my doing, I don't mind.

JAGO (*bitterly*) Don't you?

ALICE. I couldn't bear it to be because of me. Oh, I don't mind now.

JAGO (*moving above the armchair C*) I mind.

ALICE (*rising, moving to Jago and turning him to face her*) No, Paul, no. They can't hurt you. They can't touch you. You're so much bigger than they are, you can afford to laugh at them. That's why they fear you so.

JAGO. What absurd ideas you have of me. Perhaps that's where I get my own.

ALICE. What will you do, now? You can't let them reject you. Will you withdraw?

JAGO. Is that what you want me to do?

(CRAWFORD *enters* L)

CRAWFORD. Oh, I beg your pardon. Good evening, Mrs Jago.

(ALICE *exits* L, *without a word*)

Please don't let me disturb you . . .

JAGO (*holding out the paper*) Crawford. Have you seen this?

CRAWFORD (*moving to L of Jago and taking the paper*) I'm afraid I have.

(ALICE *is seen to cross outside the windows from* L *to* R)

JAGO. Can you faintly imagine what it meant to my wife to read it?

CRAWFORD. Your wife? Oh, no, surely. (*He looks after Alice. Shocked*) Jago, I very much regret that this should have happened.

(Lewis and Getliffe enter R. Lewis moves down R. Getliffe stands down R of the table up C)

JAGO. That's not enough.

CRAWFORD. I shall write to your wife personally and tell her so.

JAGO. That's not enough.

CRAWFORD. What do you expect me to do?

JAGO. Discover how and why it came into her hands. I may tell you it was deliberately sent.

CRAWFORD. You exaggerate my responsibility. I'm sincerely sorry your wife should suffer through anything in which I am even remotely concerned, but I don't consider it my duty to become a private detective.

JAGO. This attack on my wife is intended to make me withdraw.

CRAWFORD. I can't express any view on intentions in which I'm not interested.

JAGO. If you're not interested, your supporters may be.

CRAWFORD. I doubt it.

JAGO. I shall protect my wife in all ways open to reason, but while any of my colleagues are prepared to give me their votes, I shall remain a candidate for the Mastership.

(The first bell is heard pealing for dinner)

CRAWFORD. That is your privilege. *(He moves to the door L and opens it)* Are you coming into Hall, Jago?

JAGO. No. I shall dine with my wife.

(JAGO exits L)

CRAWFORD *(moving LC)* The danger with any group of men like a college is that we tend to get on each others' nerves.

LEWIS. I'm glad he spoke to you.

(JAGO is seen crossing outside the windows from L to R)

CRAWFORD. It's no concern of mine. I've never lent an ear to local tittle-tattle. I'm not prepared to begin now.

(NIGHTINGALE enters L)

Oh, Nightingale. It seems that Mrs Jago has come into possession of that circular of yours. Naturally, it can't have been sent to her by anyone connected with the college.

NIGHTINGALE. Is there anything to show that she wasn't looking through her husband's letters and found one that wasn't meant for her?

CRAWFORD. Apparently it *was* meant for her. It was addressed to her personally.

NIGHTINGALE. That kind of woman tends to imagine things. Especially when she's going through an awkward time of life.

CRAWFORD (*crossing below Nightingale to the door* L) Quite. However, it's an unfortunate business.

NIGHTINGALE. Extremely unfortunate.

(CRAWFORD *exits* L. *The sound of rain is heard as the storm breaks.* NIGHTINGALE *turns to go*)

GETLIFFE (*abruptly*) Nightingale.

(NIGHTINGALE *stops and turns*)

(*He moves* RC) Did you send that note to Jago's wife?

NIGHTINGALE. Good heavens, man, there are a dozen ways she could have read the thing accidentally.

GETLIFFE. I don't believe in that sort of accident.

(CRAWFORD *is seen outside the windows crossing from* L *to* R)

Did you send it?

NIGHTINGALE. I'm sorry, Getliffe. I'm not prepared to be cross-examined.

GETLIFFE. And I'm not prepared to let you evade the issue.

NIGHTINGALE. And if I refuse to answer?

GETLIFFE. I shall draw the obvious conclusion.

NIGHTINGALE. Conclude what you like.

(NIGHTINGALE *exits* L)

GETLIFFE (*crossing to* LC) That man's impossible.

LEWIS (*moving* RC) He's done us a service. We're on the same side again, aren't we?

GETLIFFE. Oh, no, Lewis. No, I'm not crossing over. I'm committed to Crawford. I'm sure I'm right.

LEWIS. Are you?

(NIGHTINGALE *is seen crossing outside the windows from* L *to* R)

GETLIFFE (*looking after Nightingale; troubled*) Damn!

LEWIS. Francis, do one thing.

GETLIFFE. What?

LEWIS (*deliberately*) Keep an open mind.

(GETLIFFE *hesitates. The dinner bell peals. The* FELLOWS, *wearing their gowns, are seen crossing outside the windows from* L *to* R *in the pouring rain on their way to Hall.* WINSLOW *is first. He is followed by* CHRYSTAL *and* BROWN, *then* CALVERT, PILBROW *and* LUKE)

GETLIFFE. Let's go and eat, shall we?

GETLIFFE *and* LEWIS *exit* L.

DESPARD-SMITH *goes past the windows under a large umbrella.* GAY *hurries after him and reaches the shelter of the umbrella. The two aged* ACADEMICS *exit* R *together as—*

the CURTAIN *falls*

To face page 67—The Masters, Act III, Scene 2

Photo by Houston Rogers

SCENE 2

SCENE—*The same. A fortnight later. Morning.*

When the CURTAIN *rises, the room looks ordered and immaculate. The three armchairs* RC, C *and* LC, *and the two occasional tables have been removed. The desk is turned parallel with the wall* L. *The long table, with the aid of additional tables, has been arranged to form three sides of a square and is covered with a rich cloth. Silver inkstands stand on the right and left-hand sections. Thirteen upright chairs are set at the table, seven above it and three each* R *and* L *of it.* BIDWELL *and* STRAKER *are finishing the preparations.* BIDWELL, *at the down* R *end of the table has sheets of paper and wineglasses on a tray. He moves round, setting a sheet of paper and a wineglass at each place.* STRAKER *has four decanters of wine on a tray. He sets them on the table, one down* R, *one up* R, *one* RC *and one up* L.

BIDWELL. I thought you were a boy who liked a flutter.

STRAKER. I might be. I might be. What are the odds?

BIDWELL. Well, let's see now. I'll give you two to one—Jago, two to one—Crawford, twenty to one—the field.

STRAKER (*putting his tray on the table* C *and moving to the desk*) You're not sticking your neck out, are you? (*He collects a carafe of water from the desk and puts it up* L *of the table*)

BIDWELL. It's tight, this is. Very tight.

STRAKER. Yes, I know, but . . .

BIDWELL. Ssh!

(LEWIS *enters* L. *Like all the fellows in this final scene, he wears full academic regalia.* STRAKER *goes to the desk and collects an inkstand and a gavel*)

Good morning, sir.

STRAKER. Good morning, sir.

LEWIS (*moving above the table*) Good morning, Bidwell. 'Morning, Straker.

BIDWELL. So the great old day has arrived at last, sir.

LEWIS. Yes.

(STRAKER *sets the inkstand and gavel* C *of the table and picks up his tray*)

BIDWELL (*now up* L *of the table*) I know it's wrong of us to talk among ourselves, sir, but we've had a good many words in the buttery about who's to be the next Master.

(STRAKER *moves to the table up* R *and collects a carafe of water*)

LEWIS. Have you? (*He glances at his watch and moves to the window* RC)

BIDWELL. Ten minutes to starter's orders, sir. Yes, a very popular gentleman, Dr Jago is. I should say there wasn't a servant in the college who had ever heard a word against Dr Jago.

STRAKER (*putting the carafe up* RC *on the table*) Of course, Dr Crawford is a very popular gentleman, too, sir.

(LEWIS *moves down* RC)

BIDWELL (*moving down* LC) Between ourselves, sir, I should say they were equally popular. Wouldn't you, sir?
LEWIS. Between ourselves, Bidwell, I wouldn't say anything at all.
BIDWELL. No, sir.
STRAKER. We shall drink their healths all right, sir, whoever you put in.
BIDWELL (*crossing to* R) Hear, hear!
LEWIS. Thank you, Straker. Thank you, Bidwell.
BIDWELL ⎫
STRAKER ⎭ (*together*) Thank *you*, sir.

(CALVERT *enters* L.
   STRAKER *exits* R *with his tray*)

BIDWELL. Good morning, Mr Calvert, sir.
CALVERT. 'Morning, Bidwell.

(BIDWELL *exits* R *with his tray*)

(*He crosses to Lewis*) Well, old boy, this is it. Shortly we shall have a Pope. I feel we ought to make smoke, don't you?
LEWIS. No.
CALVERT. A passing thought. I just ran into Nightingale. I gave him my deepest sympathy.
LEWIS. What for?
CALVERT. Not knowing his own mind. "It must be ghastly for you," I said. "It must make life an impossible strain," I said.
LEWIS. Not very wise.
CALVERT. Just so. But remarkably pleasing.

(LUKE *enters* L)

Hello, Walter. Ready for the fray?
LUKE. I'll be glad when this damn thing's over and I can get back to work. For the past twenty-four hours I've been lobbied by every Crawford man in the place.
LEWIS. We're doing the same to them.
LUKE. Well, everyone in this blasted college may change their minds twice a week, but I bloody well won't.

(LEWIS *turns away to the window up* RC. LUKE *crosses to* L *of Calvert*)

CALVERT. "Then up spake brave Horatio . . ."—or do I mean stout Cortez?
LUKE (*with a grin*) Stuff it!

(GAY *is seen hurrying past outside the windows from* R *to* L. *His beard*

*has been combed and his hair pomarded. He wears a red gown and hood
and carries a book)*

Gay (*off; loudly*) Here we are! Here we are!
Luke. Oh, my God!

(Luke *exits hurriedly* R)

Calvert (*moving to the window up* LC) Lewis, shall we tackle him
now?
Lewis. It's now or never. Will you start, or shall I?
Calvert. Let's make it a pincer movement. Attack on both
flanks.

(Gay *enters* L)

Gay. Good morning, good morning. Well, the great day has
dawned. The magic moment is almost upon us. (*He crosses and stands*
C, *above the table*)

(Lewis *moves to* R *of Gay.* Calvert *moves to* L *of him*)

Is everything in order? I must inspect the arrangements. Pen, paper,
wine for the toast. Capital! Wine. Yes, I think I'll take a glass before
we start. (*He pours a drink*) To warm the bones, you understand. (*He
sips his wine*)

(Lewis *and* Calvert *exchange glances*)

Lewis. Er—Professor—we very much wanted your advice . . .
Gay. Do you know what this is? My new book. (*He waves the book
at them*) Advice? I'll give you a piece of advice. Satisfy the scholars
first, show them that you're better than any of them. But when
you've become an authority, don't neglect the man in the street.
Why, I should welcome my books being presented by the films. I
don't despise these modern methods. Fine films my sagas would
make. Nothing namby-pamby about my sagas.
Calvert. No, indeed. About the election . . .
Lewis. You're occupying an exceptional position. You're the
great scholar of the College.
Calvert. The greatest Icelandic scholar of the age.
Gay. Quite so.
Lewis. We need a lead.
Calvert. Which only you can give.
Lewis. We're extremely worried.
Calvert. We want you to advise us.
Lewis. On the two candidates.
Calvert. Crawford and Jago.
Lewis. We want you to show us how to form a judgement. I
believe you've promised to support Crawford.
Gay. Have I? Yes, I recollect indicating support for Crawford.

(*He moves to the up* L *end of the table. Shrewdly*) And you two want me to change my mind, is that it?

CALVERT. Well, you're not far off the mark.

GAY. Aha! You see, you can't pull wool over my eyes.

LEWIS. We want you to think again about those two, while there's still time. You do remember them, don't you?

GAY. Of course I remember them. Jago—that's our Senior Tutor. He's not taken quite enough care of himself lately. He's lost hair and put on weight. And Crawford. He's a scientist. (*He moves to the notice-board*) A sound man, they tell me.

CALVERT. How do you feel about Jago?

GAY. Jago? He's a sound man, too.

LEWIS (*crossing to* R *of Gay*) Do you want a scientist as Master? Crawford's field is a long way from yours.

GAY (*at once*) I should never give a second's thought to such a question. (*He crosses to* C) I have never attached any importance to boundary lines between branches of learning. A man can do distinguished work in any. We ought to have outgrown these arts and science controversies before we leave the school debating society.

CALVERT (*moving to* R *of Gay*) Yes, well, at present you're in a unique position. Without you, each man has six votes. If it's understood that you vote for Crawford, the election is just a formality. The whole thing is cut and dried.

GAY. "Cut and dried"? "Cut and dried"? I don't like the sound of "Cut and dried".

LEWIS (*moving to* L *of Gay*) It means its all over bar the ceremony.

GAY. I certainly indicated support for Crawford.

LEWIS. Need that be final? After all, unlike the rest of us, you've been able to survey the whole position from on high.

GAY. Ah! Those old gods looked down from Odin's Hall.

(*They laugh*)

CALVERT. Quite so.

LEWIS. Mightn't it be best to stand aloof—and then in your own good time decide the election one way or the other?

CALVERT. What's wanted is a judgement of Solomon.

GAY (*not to be bluffed*) You're trying to bamboozle me into voting for Jago.

CALVERT. Of course we are. Will you?

GAY. I won't give you an undertaking. But the election mustn't be taken for granted. No, our founding fathers, in their wisdom, did not lay it down for us to meet in convocation just to take an election for granted. (*He crosses down* L *of the table*) Why, we might just as well send our votes by post.

LEWIS. Then you'll think of Jago?

GAY. I shall certainly think of Jago. Yes. I shall also think of Crawford. Ah. Solomon—he was a sound man, too.

(GAY *exits* L)

LEWIS. What do you think?
CALVERT. I think he'll vote for Solomon.

(JAGO *enters* R)

LEWIS (*moving down* C; *to Jago*) Don't hope too much, but it's not lost.
JAGO (*his face instantly lighting up*) What's happened?
CALVERT. We've shaken old Gay. It's not impossible he may finish on your side.
JAGO (*moving down* RC) Gay?
LEWIS (*crossing to* R *of Calvert*) He may not, but it's worth holding on for.
JAGO. But that's wonderful news! That's absolutly wonderful news!

(CHRYSTAL *enters* L)

(*He crosses to Chrystal*) Have you heard? Have you heard? Gay's come over! They think we've got Gay.
LEWIS. It's not absolutely certain.
CALVERT. I'll lay you four to one, if he can think of anyone's name but his own, he'll vote for Jago.
JAGO (*turning to Calvert and Lewis*) Marvellous! Simply marvellous! We've got the election in our hands.
CHRYSTAL (*quietly*) No.
JAGO. I can sense it. I feel suddenly nothing can stop us. (*He turns to Chrystal and becomes aware of Chrystal's expression*) What is it? What's happened? Well, tell me—don't just . . .
CHRYSTAL (*to Lewis and Calvert*) Will you leave us alone, please. (*He moves to* R *of the desk*)

(LEWIS *and* CALVERT *exit* R)

(*He moves to* L *of Jago. Carefully*) Jago, I've just come from Crawford. I've been with him two hours. He's been giving me his views on the College. I like them. With five new science Fellowships and Crawford in the Lodge, I can see this College taking the biggest jump forward it's ever made. We must move with the times. I'm sorry, Jago, but today we must have Crawford.

(*There is a pause*)

JAGO. It's the benefaction. It's because of the benefaction, isn't it?
CHRYSTAL. Partly. We need the money, and if you're Master we might not get it.
JAGO (*feverishly*) Chrystal, I'll accept Timberlake's scheme—just as it stands—the science Fellowships—everything—I'll make the plan work.

CHRYSTAL (*moving* L) It's not just that.

JAGO. We'll work it together. I'm prepared to leave certain things in the College to you. You know you don't want Crawford—you've always disliked him.

CHRYSTAL. I did. It was my mistake.

JAGO (*moving to* R *of Chrystal*) Chrystal! Royce wanted me to have it. He said—these were his very words—"I hope you get it." You liked Royce. You trusted his judgement. Doesn't that mean anything to you?

CHRYSTAL. Jago—I think Crawford will make a better Master than you. If I think that, you wouldn't expect me to vote for you.

JAGO (*fiercely*) I do expect it.

CHRYSTAL. I'm sorry. I've changed my mind. (*He moves to the door* L)

JAGO. You were the first to condemn Nightingale for doing just that.

CHRYSTAL (*stopping and turning*) All right, if it makes it easier for you, let's say that each man has the right to vote as he chooses. (*He turns and opens the door*)

JAGO. Suppose I vote as I choose? Suppose I make it impossible for Crawford to be Master?

CHRYSTAL. I don't understand.

JAGO. Suppose I abstain?

(CHRYSTAL *slams the door shut and moves to* L *of Jago*)

CHRYSTAL. You can't do that. You promised to vote for Crawford.

JAGO. You promised to vote for me.

CHRYSTAL. That's not the same thing.

JAGO. It's precisely the same.

CHRYSTAL (*moving down* L) Jago, it's too late now for an ethical argument . . .

JAGO. You spent two hours with Crawford. (*He moves to* R *of Chrystal*) Give me five minutes. Five minutes—that's all I ask.

CHRYSTAL. There isn't time. The election is almost due to start and, anyway, it will make no difference.

JAGO. Of course it will. Look, my dear Charles, this is all an absurd misunderstanding. It's my fault. I should have asked you to come and see me before. The Master and the Dean must work together. Between them they run the College, don't they? I shan't make that mistake again. I shall always come to you and especially over these new science Fellowships—you misunderstood me there. I welcome them. It will be important to have a scientist in high office. I see that now. There's the Senior Tutorship—Brown doesn't have to have it. Do you think it could go to Crawford or Getliffe?

CHRYSTAL. Now look, Jago . . .

JAGO. Well, we can discuss it later—but that's the kind of appointment where I shall look to you for advice. I shall discuss everything with you, and whatever suggestions you have to make, why, they'll be welcome, my dear man, welcome. You must be the first to dine with me in the Lodge.

(CHRYSTAL *moves to the desk* L)

We can do so much together, you and I.

(BROWN *enters* L)

Ah, there you are, Arthur. The Dean's been having last-minute doubts about me——

(BROWN *moves up* L *of the table*)

—the Dean of all people, can you imagine? But it's all right, now—isn't it, Dean?

CHRYSTAL (*moving down* L *of Brown*) Jago, are you seriously saying that if I vote for Crawford you'll abstain?

JAGO. Why not?

BROWN (*startled*) What's that?

CHRYSTAL. Man, you *can't* want me to vote for you on *those* grounds.

JAGO. Try me. You vote before me, remember?

(CHRYSTAL *exits* L *without a word*)

BROWN. Paul, you can't do that.

(*The clock strikes ten*)

JAGO (*moving to* R *of the desk*) It won't be necessary. I've cracked the whip. He'll come to heel.

BROWN (*moving to* R *of Jago*) Whatever he does, if you break your word, people will say that in your place, Crawford would never have done so. They'll say this was the final proof they were right all the time.

JAGO. Do *you* think they've been right all the time?

BROWN. I'm as sure they are wrong as I've ever been.

JAGO. You're asking me to sign my own rejection. To watch another man sit where I should have sat, to put him there myself—and to call him Master. (*He sits at the desk*)

(WINSLOW, PILBROW, GETLIFFE *and* NIGHTINGALE *cross outside the windows from* R *to* L)

No, no, I can't do it. I just can't do it. I won't, Arthur. I won't. (*He covers his face with his hands*)

BROWN. Paul! Pull yourself together, man. Paul, they're coming. (*He stands between Jago and the other fellows as they enter*)

(LUKE, LEWIS *and* CALVERT *enter up* R.
CHRYSTAL *enters* L *and holds the door open.*

GAY *and* DESPARD-SMITH *enter* L. GAY *carries his book and a copy of the statutes.*

WINSLOW, PILBROW, GETLIFFE *and* NIGHTINGALE *next enter* L. LUKE *crosses and sits on the downstage chair* L *of the table.* CALVERT *sits on the downstage chair* R *of the table.* LEWIS *and* GETLIFFE *meet* C, *below the table and look at each other for a moment, then* LEWIS *sits above Luke at* L *of the table and* GETLIFFE *sits above Calvert at* R *of the table.* GAY *sits* C, *above the table, with* PILBROW R *of him and* DESPARD-SMITH L *of him.* WINSLOW *sits* R *of Pilbrow, above the table.* NIGHTIN-GALE *sits above Lewis at* L *of the table.* CHRYSTAL *moves to the window* LC *and closes it, then crosses and sits above Getliffe at* R *of the table.* BROWN *moves and sits above the table, at the left end of it.* JAGO *rises, follows Brown and sits* R *of him, above the table.*

CRAWFORD *enters* L *and crosses above the table to* R)

CRAWFORD (*to Gay; equably*) I apologize if I'm late, Senior Fellow. (*He slips into the vacant seat* R *of Winslow, above the table*)

(*As the last stroke of ten dies away,* GAY *struggles to his feet*)

GAY. Gentlemen, I bid you good morning.

(*The others murmur "Good morning"*)

Before we begin, I have a small presentation to make. I wish to present to the society, for inclusion in the library, this copy of my latest publication. I hope, indeed I expect that most Fellows have already bought it. (*He looks keenly at Jago*) I take it you've bought yours, Jago?

JAGO (*abstractedly*) Mm? Yes, I have a copy.

GAY (*looking keenly at Crawford*) And you, Crawford? What about you?

CRAWFORD. Er—no. As a matter of fact, I haven't—yet.

GAY (*significantly*) Ah. Indeed.

CALVERT. The judgement of Solomon.

GAY. What was that?

CALVERT. An irrelevant observation, sir. I apologize.

GAY. I congratulate you. Gentlemen, I now propose to carry out my statutory duties. (*He opens his leather-covered copy of the statutes, clears his throat and reads*) "At ten o'clock in the morning of the appointed day, the Fellows shall assemble in convocation to elect a Master, that Fellow who is first in order of precedence presiding." This is the appointed day, no doubt about that. And I am the Fellow first in order of precedence. No doubt about that, either. So now is the time to do my duty. In accordance with Statute B, paragraph nine, I call upon you all to rise——

(*The others all rise*)

—and to repeat after me: "I do hereby declare that, having full knowledge of the statutes——"

OMNES. "I do hereby declare that, having full knowledge of the statutes——"

GAY. "——and without thought of gain or loss or worldly considerations whatsoever——"

OMNES. "——and without thought of gain or loss or worldly considerations whatsoever——"

GAY. "——I will now choose as Master . . ."

WINSLOW. Must I stand here and spout this archaic effusion?

GAY (*shocked*) I beg your pardon?

WINSLOW. Is all this necessary?

GAY. Most certainly. You will comply with the statutes.

WINSLOW. I do so under protest.

GAY. Your protest is noted—and quashed. Where were we?

BROWN. "——I will now choose as Master——"

GAY. "——I will now choose as Master that man who, in my belief——"

OMNES. "——I will now choose as Master that man, who, in my belief——"

GAY. "——will best maintain the well-being and glory of the College——"

OMNES. "——will best maintain the well-being and glory of the College——"

GAY. "——and this I vow in sincerity and truth."

OMNES. "——and this I vow in sincerity and truth."

GAY. Well done. Kindly be seated.

(*All except* GAY *resume their seats*)

I am now about to call upon you to cast your votes for the Mastership. To do this, you will write your own name and that of the fellow of your choice upon the piece of paper in front of you, in accordance with Statute C, paragraph five. Having done so, you will each in turn rise and in a clear voice make your declaration, beginning with the Junior Fellow and so on up the line in order of seniority, until we reach the Senior Fellow, who is, of course, myself. I have asked the Dean and the Tutor to act as tellers, so that there shall be no mistakes. Is all clear? Despard, have you grasped the statutes?

DESPARD-SMITH. I k-know them by heart.

GAY. What about you, Winslow?

WINSLOW. Yes, yes. Let's get on.

GAY. We are getting on, we are getting on. But the correct procedure must be observed.

WINSLOW. I have never believed in multiplying mummery.

GAY. Mummery is one thing, tradition another. Gentlemen, charge your glasses.

(CALVERT, CRAWFORD, BROWN *and* DESPARD-SMITH *fill their glasses first then pass the decanters along the table to* R)

(*When all glasses are filled*) I give you the toast to the College, in the

F

words first spoken by our pious founder in the year of our Lord, thirteen hundred and eighty-six. "May ye who strive and study here do so even as comrades and brothers, being united one with an-other."

WINSLOW. A manifest absurdity.

GAY (*raising his glass*) Gentlemen—the College!

(*The others rise*)

OMNES. The College!

(*They drink, then all except* GAY *resume their seats*)

GAY. And now, gentlemen, the great moment. I call upon you to cast your votes for the Mastership of our beloved College. Do even as your conscience guides you, and may Providence direct your thoughts. (*He sits*)

(*There is silence as all the* FELLOWS, *except* JAGO, *write their votes.* GAY *finishes last.* JAGO *sits motionless*)

Are we all done? Capital! I now call upon you each, in turn, to rise and without fear or favour to declare yourselves. Are the Dean and Tutor ready?

CHRYSTAL ⎱
BROWN   ⎰ (*together*) Yes.

GAY. Junior Fellow.

LUKE (*rising and reading*) "I, Walter John Luke, vote for Dr Paul Jago." (*He sits*)

BROWN. One vote for Dr Jago.

CALVERT (*rising and reading*) "I, Roy Clement Edward Calvert, elect Paul Jago." (*He sits*)

BROWN. Two votes for Dr Jago.

LEWIS (*rising and reading*) "I, Lewis Stephen Eliot, elect Paul Jago." (*He sits*)

BROWN. Three votes for Dr Jago.

GETLIFFE (*rising and reading*) "I, Francis Ernest Getliffe, elect Redvers Thomas Arbuthnot Crawford." (*He sits*)

CHRYSTAL. One vote for Dr Crawford.

BROWN. Three for Dr Jago.

NIGHTINGALE (*rising and reading*) "Ronald Edmund Alexander Nightingale votes for Dr Crawford." (*He sits*)

CHRYSTAL. Two votes for Dr Crawford.

BROWN. Three for Dr Jago.

CHRYSTAL (*rising and reading*) "I, Charles Percy Chrystal elect Dr Thomas Crawford." (*He sits*)

(*There are murmurs of astonishment from the* FELLOWS. GAY *bangs his gavel for silence*)

Three votes for Dr Crawford.

BROWN. Three for Dr Jago. (*He rises and reads*) "I, Arthur Brown, elect Paul Jago." (*He sits*) Four votes for Dr Jago.

CHRYSTAL. Three for Dr Crawford.

CRAWFORD (*rising and reading*) "I, Redvers Thomas Arbuthnot Crawford choose Paul Jago to be Master of this College." (*He sits*)

BROWN. Five votes for Dr Jago.

CHRYSTAL. Three for Dr Crawford.

(*There is a pause. The others look at Jago*)

BROWN (*steadily*) Paul?

(JAGO, *after a pause, rises*)

JAGO. "I, Paul Jago, elect Thomas Crawford." (*He sits, ashen*)

CHRYSTAL. Four votes for Dr Crawford.

BROWN. Five for Dr Jago.

(WINSLOW *rises, his eyes on* JAGO's *agony, then suddenly tears up his paper. The others react*)

WINSLOW. Godfrey Harold Winslow declines to vote.

(*There are murmurs of astonishment*)

GETLIFFE. What's that?

WINSLOW (*snapping*) I abstain. (*He sits abruptly*)

CHRYSTAL. But you can't abstain.

GAY (*banging his gavel*) Quiet, please. Pray continue.

DESPARD-SMITH (*rising and reading*) "Albert Theophilus Despard-Smith elects Redvers Thomas Arbuthnot C-Crawford." (*He sits*)

CHRYSTAL. Five votes for Dr Crawford.

BROWN. Five for Dr Jago.

PILBROW (*rising and reading*) "I, Eustace Pilbrow elect Redvers Thomas Arbuthnot Crawford." (*He sits*)

CHRYSTAL. Six votes for Dr Crawford.

BROWN. Five for Dr Jago.

(*There is a silence*)

GAY. Well, who's next? Seven votes elects a master. Who's next? Who are we waiting for?

WINSLOW. You.

GAY. Ah! (*He rises slowly and takes a paper from his pocket*)

(*The others react*)

(*He reads in majestic tones*) "I, Maurice Harvey Laurence Gay, Senior Fellow of the College and Emeritus Professor in the university, having performed my duties as Senior Fellow in accordance with Statutes B to F inclusive, and having examined my conscience with regard to all aspects of this matter—(*he picks up his voting paper*) do hereby give my vote for the Mastership of this college to . . ." (*He *drops his voting paper on the floor*) Ah—now where . . . ? I wonder if you'd be so kind . . . ?

(PILBROW *and* DESPARD-SMITH *scrabble on the floor.* DESPARD-SMITH *retrieves the paper and hands it to Gay*)

Thank you. Do the fellows wish me to start again?
WINSLOW. No, no. For God's sake . . .
GAY. In that case, I hereby give my vote to . . . (*He looks blankly at the paper, puzzled*)

(PILBROW *indicates the back of the paper*)

(*He turns the paper over*) Ah! (*Triumphantly*) To Dr Paul Jago. There we are. There are the votes. Who wins?
LEWIS. No-one.

(*There is an outcry from the others.* GAY *bangs his gavel*)

GAY. What's that?
LEWIS. Neither candidate has been elected.
GAY. Is that correct?
CHRYSTAL. Six votes for Dr Crawford.
BROWN. Six votes for Dr Jago.

(GAY *sits*)

GETLIFFE (*rising; grimly*) In other words, we've thrown the election of the Master of this College into the hands of the Visitor. (*He sits*)

DESPARD-SMITH		This is an absolute disaster!
CALVERT		The Dean and Pilbrow between them . . .
NIGHTINGALE	(*together*)	If Winslow hadn't lost his head . . .
LUKE		Do you mean to say we've been wasting our bloody time . . . ?

GAY (*pounding his gavel*) Order, gentlemen! Silence! You forget yourselves. Now, this is a very remarkable development. The question is, what's to be done? I must look up the statutes.
CHRYSTAL. There's no need for that. The Bursar abstained. I propose he be asked to reconsider.
LUKE (*at once*) Oh, no, you don't. He's contracted out. That's the finish.
GETLIFFE. But that means it goes to the Visitor.
LUKE. Right. Let it go.
DESPARD-SMITH. N-No! Disaster!
GAY. Quiet, Despard! I will have order.
CHRYSTAL (*rising; formally*) Senior Fellow, I move the Bursar be asked to vote again.
NIGHTINGALE (*rising*) I second that.

(CHRYSTAL *sits*)

LUKE (*rising*) In that case I move we all vote again. Anyone second that?

CALVERT (*rising*) Yes, I will. (*He sits*)

NIGHTINGALE. That's ridiculous, Luke . . .

LUKE. I don't give a damn. What's good for the goose is good for the gander. (*He sits*)

(NIGHTINGALE *sits*)

GETLIFFE. But if we all vote again, we'll be back where we started.

LEWIS. Not necessarily. Someone else may cross over.

NIGHTINGALE. They won't.

PILBROW. I might.

(*There is general reaction*)

BROWN		What?
GETLIFFE	(*together*)	Oh, for God's sake, Eustace . . .
DESPARD-SMITH		Disaster! I w-wash my hands . . .

CHRYSTAL (*rising; grimly*) There's a motion on the table that Mr Winslow be asked to vote again. Winslow . . .

WINSLOW. I refuse to be drawn.

(CHRYSTAL *sits*)

GAY (*rising*) Gentlemen, in view of this totally unexpected result —I hereby declare this election null and . . .

PILBROW (*quickly*) No, no, Gay, you can't do that. You'll make the whole College a laughing-stock.

GAY. I'm in the hands of the meeting. (*He sits*)

CHRYSTAL (*rising; loudly*) I demand that my motion be put. The Bursar must be made to vote.

LUKE. I demand that my motion be put. We must all vote again.

CALVERT		Chrystal. How on earth do you think you can persuade the Bursar to change his mind?
LEWIS		Why should he?
GETLIFFE	(*together*)	Winslow—listen to reason.
BROWN		Well said!
CHRYSTAL		No.
PILBROW		You can't *make* a man vote.

JAGO (*jumping to his feet*) No! No! For God's sake, stop! This can't happen.

(CHRYSTAL *sits*)

PILBROW		Paul, my dear fellow, sit down.
NIGHTINGALE		This is fantastic behaviour.
BROWN	(*together*)	Paul, sit down, you're not helping yourself . . .
DESPARD-SMITH		We really can't allow . . .

GAY (*banging his gavel*) Order, order! Dr Jago, I must ask you to sit down.

JAGO. Look, don't you see it doesn't matter? However he votes doesn't matter now. It just won't do.

GETLIFFE   } (*together*)   { What on earth do you mean by that?
CHRYSTAL   }   { I really think you should be quiet, Jago.

NIGHTINGALE (*rising*) Gay, can't you control the meeting? Make the fool sit down. (*He sits*)

LUKE (*half-rising and turning to Nightingale*) My God, you're an offensive bastard!

(LEWIS *pulls* LUKE *down on to his seat*)

DESPARD-SMITH. Gentlemen! G-Gentlemen!

GAY (*pounding his gavel*) Unless the meeting comes to order I shall declare it adjourned forthwith.

CALVERT. Why can't we hear Jago?

BROWN. Yes, Gay, let him speak.

NIGHTINGALE. I'm damned if I see why. He knows how Winslow would vote and if he hasn't the dignity to face it . . .

WINSLOW (*rising; snapping*) He knows nothing of the kind. Neither do you.

(JAGO *sits. There is a general outburst*)

GETLIFFE		(*to Nightingale*) And what's more, if you stay quiet for two minutes we might. . .
CALVERT		You're not helping anyone, Nightingale.
LEWIS		Sit down and keep quiet. He's got every right to vote as he chooses.
CHRYSTAL	(*together*)	We'll never get anywhere at this rate.
		(WINSLOW *glares at the others*)
PILBROW		It was you who put up Crawford, anyway.
		(GAY *hammers vaguely with his gavel*)
DESPARD-SMITH		Please! Gentlemen!
NIGHTINGALE		Then he shouldn't have stood in the first place.
WINSLOW		Sit down!

CRAWFORD (*rising suddenly; with calm authority*) Gentlemen!

(*The meeting quietens at once.* NIGHTINGALE *sits*)

(*He turns to Gay*) Senior Fellow—with respect—speaking both as a member of the electoral body and as a fellow-candidate, if Dr Jago wishes to address the College, I think it should hear what he has to say. (*He sits*)

GAY. Are there any objections?

NIGHTINGALE. Yes. I object strongly.

GAY. Does anyone other than Dr Nightingale object?

(*There is no reply*)

Dr Jago.

(JAGO *rises*)

JAGO (*after a pause; carefully and with rigid control*) You *must* vote again—all of you—and you *must* vote unanimously.

NIGHTINGALE. Have you got the damned impertinence to say we must all vote for you?

GETLIFFE. Oh, for God's sake, Nightingale . . .

GAY (*to Nightingale*) If you speak again, I shall ask you to leave the meeting.

JAGO. I will answer Nightingale. (*He continues fastidiously, choosing his words with the utmost care*) Ever since the day Vernon Royce was brought back to the Lodge to die, the craving to be Master of this College has not left me. I had lived with the hope of it for years, but as something far off, a distant possibility—until these last weeks, when suddenly to be Master became not only possible but probable. It was not just that I was avid for office. It went beyond that. I told myself there were things that only I could do, that I had intimations others could not begin to hear. I saw the College in years to come looking back on my time and saying, "Jago—he was the greatest of the Masters." As the election drew near, I became increasingly indignant and astonished that there could be any opposition to me as Master of this college. I was this College. This College was I, Paul Jago. (*He pauses*) Ambition can do many things to a man. Not the least is to make him ridiculous. No one man can be a college, any more than one man can be a nation, or anything but one man. If he tries he abandons everything he stood for as I have in these last weeks. Everything. My work, my friends, my wife. My wife has been humiliated—through me—because of me. I see all this now, clearly. Yet here's the appalling thing. If I were elected, I should lose sight of it again. I know it. Even now I would like to hear you call me "Master" . . . So there is nothing more for me to do—except, of course, withdraw from this election. (*He sits*)

BROWN } (*together*) { Paul, you're making a great mistake!
LUKE } { Don't be a damned fool, Jago!

JAGO (*with finality*) I *withdraw*.

(*There is a silence then GAY rises slowly*)

GAY. There is one candidate for the Mastership. So I shall not call for a written vote. Will those fellows who support the election of Dr Crawford please stand?

(*The other* FELLOWS, *with the exception of* CRAWFORD, *rise one after the other in the following order.* GETLIFFE *first, then* CHRYSTAL, PILBROW, DESPARD-SMITH, NIGHTINGALE, JAGO, LEWIS, WINSLOW, LUKE, CALVERT *and finally* BROWN)

Thank you. Please be seated.

(*The others sit*)

(*He turns to Crawford*) Dr Redvers Thomas Arbuthnot Crawford.

(CRAWFORD *rises*)

I declare you this day elected Master of this College and I give the College into your charge. (*He sits*)
CRAWFORD (*calmly*) I thank you, Senior Fellow. I thank the College. (*He sits*)
GAY (*picking up his glass*) And now I have just one last duty . . .
JAGO. Senior Fellow, with your permission . . .

(GAY *looks enquiringly at Jago.* PILBROW *plucks at Gay's elbow and whispers to him*)

GAY. Ah. Yes, indeed.

(JAGO *rises slowly, glass in hand*)

JAGO (*after a pause*) Gentlemen—the Master! (*He raises his glass to Crawford*)

(*All except* CRAWFORD *rise*)

OMNES. The Master!

The toast is drunk as—

the CURTAIN *falls*

FURNITURE AND PROPERTY LIST

ACT I

SCENE I

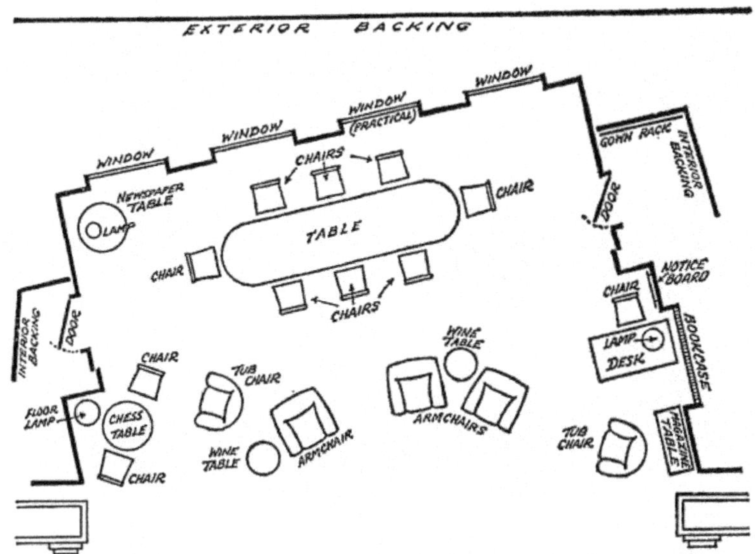

On stage: Long mahogany table. *On it:* silver tray with decanter of port,
  12 glasses, ashtrays, bowl of nuts, nut crackers
  11 upright chairs
  Tub chair (down R)
  Tub chair (down L)
  Small table (down R) *On it:* chess-board and chess-men
  Standard lamp (down R)
  Table (up R) *On it:* newspapers, magazines, table-lamp
  Writing-desk (L) *On it:* blotter, inkstand, pens, etc., table-lamp,
  ashtray, writing paper
  Table (down L) *On it:* magazines
  On wall L: notice-board and notices
  Built-in bookshelves (L) *In them:* books
  3 pairs electric-candle wall-brackets
  Window curtains
  Carpet on floor
  2 occasional tables. *On them:* ashtrays
  3 leather armchairs (RC, C and LC)
  Light switches below door L
Windows closed
Doors closed
Window curtains open
Light fittings on

Personal: Brown: lighted cigarette, watch
Jago: hat and coat
Winslow: gown and mortar-board
Pilbrow: gown, pencil
Newby: top hat

Scene 2

Strike: Dirty glasses
Decanter
Bowl of nuts

Set: 12 clean glasses
Full decanter of port
On table down R: newspaper
Tidy room generally
Windows closed
Window curtains closed
Doors closed
Light fittings on

ACT II

Scene 1

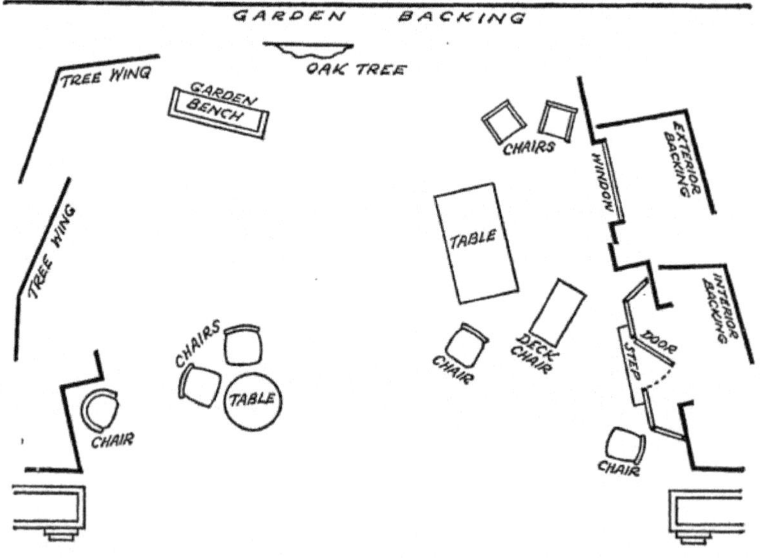

On stage: Buffet-table (LC) *On it:* white cloth, bowl of punch, ladle, box of
matches
Round garden table (RC)

       7 upright garden chairs
       Garden seat (up RC)
House door open
Lights on in house

Off stage : Tray. *On it :* 12 glasses (MRS ROYCE)
           2 cushions (JOAN)
           Deck-chair (CALVERT)
           Bunch of flowers (ALICE)
           Box of cigars (CALVERT)
           2 ashtrays (JOAN)
           Table-lighter (JOAN)
           Cigar (CRAWFORD)
           Cigar (SIR HORACE)
           Glass of claret (WINSLOW)

SCENE 2

Setting as at the end of the previous scene

Off stage : Cigar (CRAWFORD)

ACT III

SCENE 1

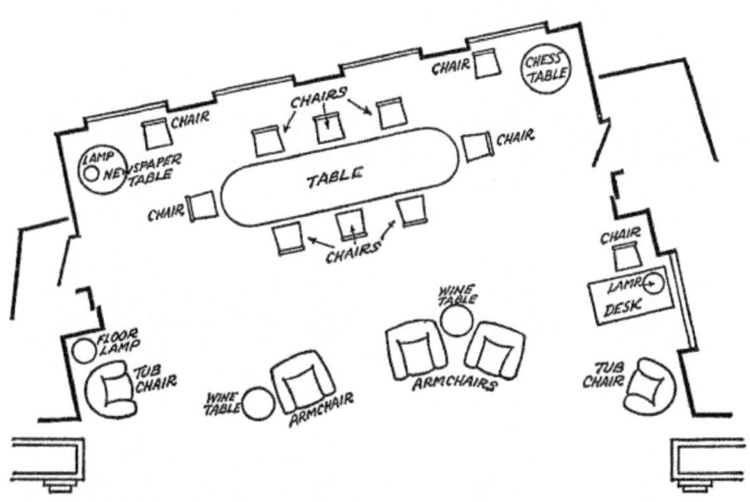

Setting as Act I

Strike: Table down L
Move table down R to corner up L
Move one upright chair from R to R of table up L
Move one upright chair down R to L of table up R
Move tub chair RC to wall down R
Move tub chair L to corner down L

Set: *On dining-table:* silver tray, silver pot with tea, 12 cups, 12 saucers, 12 teaspoons, sugar, milk, 12 small plates, 12 small knives, 12 napkins, lemon curd tarts, cake, buns, etc.

Window LC open
Window curtains open
Doors closed
Light fittings off

Off stage: Examination results (BROWN)
Examination results (DESPARD-SMITH)
Tray (BIDWELL)
Tray (STRAKER)
Hold-all (PILBROW)
Crumb tray and brush (BIDWELL)
Tray. *On it:* bottle of whisky, syphon of soda, glass (BIDWELL)
Umbrella (DESPARD-SMITH)

Personal: WINSLOW: notice
GAY: fountain pen
CHRYSTAL: letter
ALICE: handbag. *In it:* letter

SCENE 2

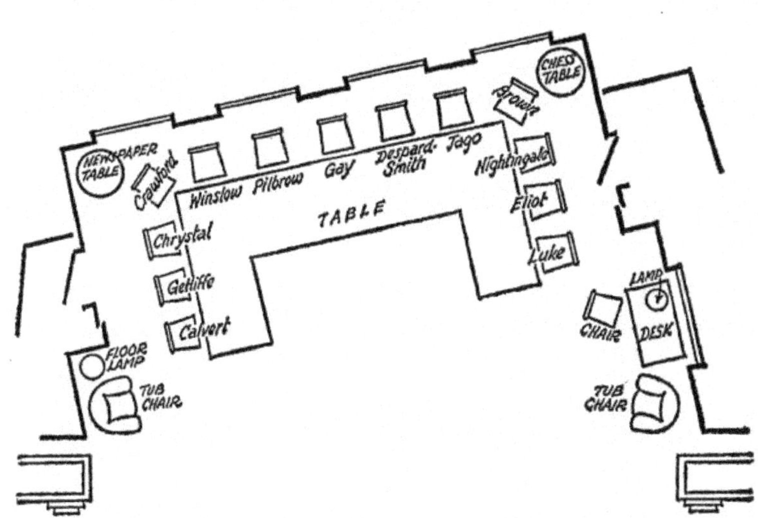

Strike: Everything from table up C
           Armchairs RC, C and LC
           2 occasional tables
Turn desk L parallel to wall L with desk chair R of it

Set: Tables to form three sides of square
        13 upright chairs at table: 7 above it, 3 each R and L of it
        On table: cloth, 2 silver inkstands, 1 each R and L
        On desk: silver inkstand, 13 pencils, gavel, carafe of water
        On table R: carafe of water
Window LC open
Doors open
Window curtains open
Light fittings on

Off stage: Tray. *On it:* 13 sheets of paper, 13 wineglasses (BIDWELL)
              Tray. *On it:* 4 decanters of wine (STRAKER)
              Book (GAY)
              Copy of Statutes (GAY)

Personal: LEWIS: watch
             GAY: piece of paper

LIGHTING PLOT

Property fittings required: 3 pairs electric-candle wall-brackets, standard
lamp, 2 table-lamps

ACT I, Scene 1. Interior. A large room. Evening
>The Apparent Sources of Light are, in daytime, large windows
>in the back wall; and at night, 3 wall-brackets up RC, up C and
>up LC, a table-lamp up R, a table-lamp L and a standard lamp
>down R

>The Main Acting Areas are the whole stage

To open: Light fittings on
Dusk outside windows

No cues

ACT I, Scene 2. Evening

To open: Light fittings on
Light from exterior lamp outside windows

Cue 1   Lewis switches out lights   (Page 23)
Snap out all fittings
Snap out covering lights

Cue 2   Brown switches on lights   (Page 24)
Snap in all fittings
Snap in covering lights

ACT II, Scene 1. Exterior/interior. A garden and house. Night
>The Apparent Sources of Light are moonlight and artificial light in
>the house L
>The Main Acting Areas are RC, C, LC and down L

To open: Effect of bright moonlight
Lights on in house L

No cues

ACT II, Scene 2. The garden. Night

To open: Lights as at the end of the previous scene
No cues

ACT III, Scene 1. The Combination Room. Late afternoon

To open: Effect of dull daylight
Fittings off

Cue 3   Straker switches on lights   (Page 60)
Snap in fittings
Snap in covering lights

ACT III, Scene 2. The Combination Room. Morning

To open: Effect of sunshine
Fittings off

No cues

EFFECTS PLOT

ACT I

SCENE 1

Cue 1 JAGO: ". . . those one loves." (Page 2)
Church clock strikes the half-hour

Cue 2 BROWN: "Please." (Page 15)
Church clock strikes ten

SCENE 2

Cue 3 CALVERT: "Bang on the dot." (Page 23)
Church clock strikes the quarter

ACT II

SCENE 1

Cue 4 CALVERT: ". . . he sees these." (Page 32)
Sound of choir singing in the distance

Cue 5 CALVERT and JOAN drink (Page 32)
Fade singing

Cue 6 BROWN: ". . . off a miracle." (Page 43)
The church clock strikes the half-hour

SCENE 2

Cue 7 THE MASTER: ". . . a decent conversation." (Page 51)
The church clock strikes the hour

ACT III

SCENE 1

Cue 8 LEWIS: "And yours." (Page 60)
The church clock strikes six

Cue 9 JAGO: ". . . for the Mastership." (Page 65)
Bell peals for dinner

Cue 10 NIGHTINGALE: "Extremely unfortunate." (Page 66)
Sound of rain

Cue 11 LEWIS: "Keep an open mind." (Page 66)
Bell peals for dinner

SCENE 2

Cue 12 BROWN: ". . . can't do that." (Page 73)
Clock strikes ten

www.ingramcontent.com/pod-product-compliance
Ingram Content Group UK Ltd.
Pitfield, Milton Keynes, MK11 3LW, UK
UKHW021823150726
7214IPUK00017B/282